Student Wo

for

Public Speaking:
Concepts and Skills for a Diverse Society
Fourth Edition

Clella Iles Jaffe
George Fox University

Australia • Canada • Mexico • Singapore • Spain • United Kingdom • United States

Printed in the United States of America
1 2 3 4 5 6 7 07 06 05 04 03

Printer: Globus Printing

ISBN: 0-534-60653-9

For more information about our products, contact us at:
Thomson Learning Academic Resource Center
1-800-423-0563

For permission to use material from this text, contact us by:
Phone: 1-800-730-2214
Fax: 1-800-731-2215
Web: http://www.thomsonrights.com

Wadsworth/Thomson Learning
10 Davis Drive
Belmont, CA 94002-3098
USA

Asia
Thomson Learning
5 Shenton Way #01-01
UIC Building
Singapore 068808

Australia/New Zealand
Thomson Learning
102 Dodds Street
Southbank, Victoria 3006
Australia

Canada
Nelson
1120 Birchmount Road
Toronto, Ontario M1K 5G4
Canada

Europe/Middle East/South Africa
Thomson Learning
High Holborn House
50/51 Bedford Row
London WC1R 4LR
United Kingdom

Latin America
Thomson Learning
Seneca, 53
Colonia Polanco
11560 Mexico D.F.
Mexico

Spain/Portugal
Paraninfo
Calle/Magallanes, 25
28015 Madrid, Spain

CONTENTS

Welcome to public speaking, one of the oldest academic disciplines in the Western university curriculum. Rhetoric or public speaking has been taught for at least 2500 years. However, public speaking is neither outdated nor dead. Speakers continue to inform, persuade, and entertain audiences every day and on every continent of the world.

The purpose of this course is to introduce you to some of the most common forms of public speaking in the United States. Knowing how to organize your ideas and present them publicly will empower you in a culture that values communication. In addition, you'll learn about other speaking traditions—both of co-cultural groups within the United States and of global cultures. This is important in a world that is increasingly shrinking through media, immigration, international trade, and other factors that bring people from different cultural traditions face-to-face in communication events.

This course balances principles and practice in public speaking. The text presents theories, concepts, and terminology, along with models speech texts and outlines you can study. This Student Workbook contains worksheets and assignments to guide you as you put theory into practice. You won't have time in a single academic term to give every type of speech described here and in the text; however, these guidelines may be useful in your future speaking. Each assignment describes a type of speech and is followed by an evaluation form. Your instructor may use these forms to assess your grade; alternatively, you can use them as guidelines in your speech preparation.

Course Objectives

- Given a purposive public speaking situation, you will be able to prepare and deliver a speech appropriate to that situation.
- Given a purposive speaking presentation, you will be able to listen to the speeches of others and evaluate their presentations, using criteria developed in the course.
- Your understanding of both Western traditions and other speaking and listening traditions will increase, making you a more effective participant in an increasingly diverse society and world.

Instructor: ______________________________

Office Location: ______________________________

Office Hours: ______________________________

Rhetoric, I shall argue, should be a study of misunderstanding and its remedies. We struggle all our days with misunderstandings and no apology is required for any study which can prevent or remove them.

A. Richards, *Philosophy of Rhetoric*

COURSE REQUIREMENTS

Quintilian, a first century AD Roman educator, provided a detailed account of the ideal education of a public speaker. He emphasized four areas of competency necessary for a good speaker: reading, writing, listening, and speaking. These four areas serve as the focus for the requirements of most public speaking courses.

The Reading Requirements

In addition to the text, *Public Speaking: Concepts and Skills for a Diverse Society, 4/e,* by Clella Jaffe, you'll read a variety of supplementary sources as you research your speech topics. Using a variety of sources with different perspectives will help you better understand your topics. Consider reading a major newspaper such as the *New York Times* or the *Washington Post* regularly during this academic term.

Your purchase of a new text also buys you a four-month password to the InfoTrac College Edition database. There you'll find literally millions of articles on almost any topic you would choose for a classroom speech.

The Speaking Requirements

Of course, you'll give a number of public speeches in this class—your instructor will give you specific assignments regarding them. Although you will only speak a total of around 25 minutes, you may face a lot of anxiety about those few minutes! Begin now to think of topics that interest you. Read newspapers, listen to news reports, and look in your other courses for fascinating topics that you'd like to explore further. Be creative, and plan to learn a lot.

The Listening Requirements

Listening to other speakers is a vital part of learning to speak well. Modeling yourself after good speakers and avoiding the mistakes of others will make you more effective. In addition, you'll find that information from your classmates' well-prepared speeches will increase your understanding of the world in which you live.

Respectful listening to classmates is important, and as part of your classroom listening, you will probably be expected to participate in discussion of the speeches. For this reason, attendance is generally a course requirement.

The Writing Requirements

Quintilian believed that clear writing reflects clear thinking—another major goal of this course. Throughout the term, you'll have many opportunities to show your clarity of thought and your analytic skills in written assignments. These skills will help you in the world of work that often demands written as well as oral reports.

For these reasons, most instructors require speech outlines, and both the text and this resource workbook present a number of model outlines. In addition, you will probably be asked to write a speaking outline for each speech—one that contains only cue words and phrases.

You may also be asked to write in-class outlines and critiques of your fellow students' speeches. These critiques provide helpful feedback to beginning speakers.

PART I

CHAPTER-BY-CHAPTER ACTIVITIES

CHAPTER 1: INTRODUCTION TO PUBLIC SPEAKING AND CULTURE

Activity 1.1: Assessing Your Competence

This activity is similar to Stop and Check: Assess Your Current Competence located on text page 6.

In each circle identify the communication competencies you currently have in each category.

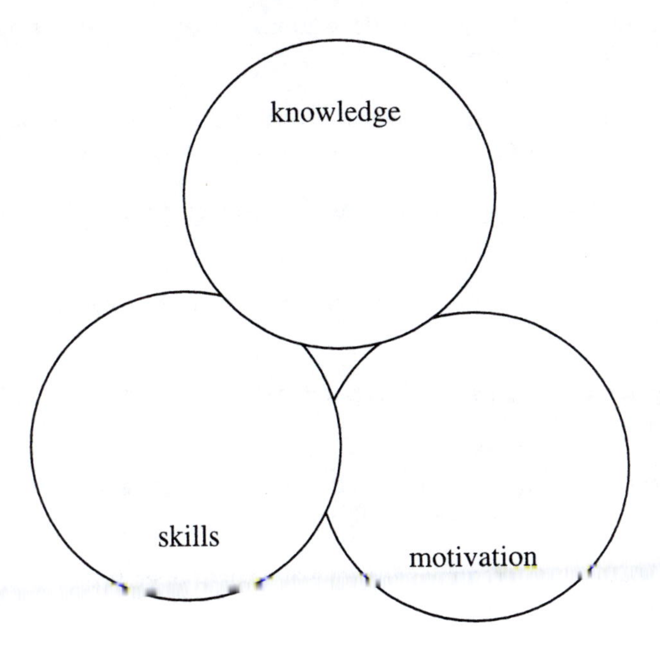

In the circles below, write the skills you want to develop in each category during this course.

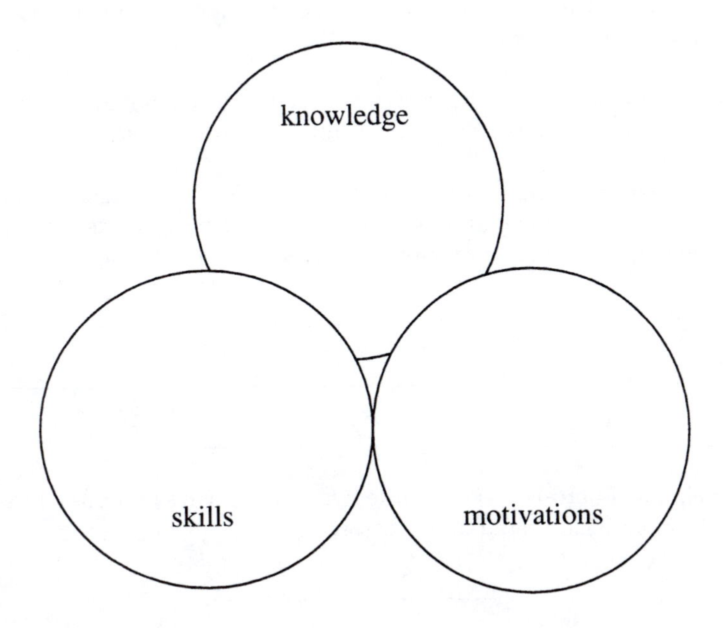

Activity 1.2: The Value of Effective Communication

Communication courses such as public speaking can benefit you in an "information society" that depends on your ability both to send and to evaluate face-to-face, print, and mediated messages. Good communication skills are important in every major profession. Here are just a few careers in which listening and speaking skills will enhance your success. Skim through the list then answer the questions below.

- **Business**. Salesperson, manager, public relations officer, negotiator, employee trainer, personnel director, consultant.
- **Public Relations/Advertising**. Publicity, advertising, marketing specialist, press agent, public opinion researcher.
- **Government**. Politician, speechwriter, campaign director, legislative assistant, lobbyist, press secretary.
- **Law**. Prosecutor, defense attorney, paralegal, legal educator, mediator, jury selection consultant.
- **Media**. Reporter, scriptwriter, producer, filmmaker, media librarian, technician, researcher, director, editor.
- **Entertainment and Arts**. Creative artist, business manager, author, promoter, public relations director, consultant, agent, fund-raiser.
- **Medicine**. Health educator, public relations director, trainer, health counselor, drug rehabilitationist.
- **Education**. Elementary, secondary, postsecondary teacher, speech pathologist, librarian, university recruiter, fund-raiser, safety educator (e.g. police officer, firefighter, park ranger, multicultural educator.)
- **Social and Human Services.** Minister, social worker, family counselor, human rights officer, community affairs specialist.
- **High Technology Industries**. Producer or technician for closed-circuit TV or teleconference, performance assessor, speech synthesizer, researcher.
- **International Arenas**. Producer of information for international audiences, foreign correspondent, educator, humanitarian worker, international corporation representative, diplomat, negotiator, international relations specialist, tour coordinator.

Which career fields interest you? ________________, ____________________, ______________________

Which specific jobs interest you? ____________________________, ____________________________,

____________________________, ______________________________________

Select a job or career field that interests you and write two or three ways that this course in public speaking will help you communicate better in that career. ______________________________

____

Activity 1.3: Mere Law, Mere Medicine, Mere Rhetoric

Don Smith, University of New Haven

Although the study of public speaking has a long--and arguably proud--tradition, the term "rhetoric" is widely used in negative ways in this culture. In this essay, which appeared in the Eastern Communication Association Newsletter, Professor Smith discusses common misconceptions of the word "rhetoric" in U. S. public discourse. (This goes with text page 7 and Exercise 5 at the end of the chapter.)

. . . Like millions of other Americans [one evening], my fiancee Barbara and I were sitting in the living room, eating dinner and watching the ABC evening news. Then Bill Redecker appeared with a report concerning American companies who recently struck successful business deals with Japan. "Reason not rhetoric," he announced, resulted in lucrative contracts with the Japanese.

What must viewers have thought? Whew?! Good thing those business leaders were smart enough to avoid rhetoric, that media buzz word denoting mere, shallow, empty, flowery, bombastic, superficial, not to be trusted, spur of the moment, grab bag, tired, worn out, other than what he/she really meant, kind of speech. When rhetoric appears in the media, more often than not it is drawn in caricature, big mouth, small brain, dumbo ears and beady eyes, just short of a clown hat and funny nose--a sad disposition for a term whose roots can be traced to the start of Western Civilization.

Worldwide there are thousands of people who have had formal training in the practice and analysis of rhetoric, a field that like medicine involves both science and art. In graduate classes these people have heard and now profess as did Aristotle, that rhetoric is the "faculty of observing in any given case all the available means of persuasion," that proper rhetorical practice is the result of ethical character, sound logic, and the appropriate use of emotional appeals; that each rhetor is duty bound to know her subject and audience thoroughly, to find the right arguments and proofs, and to adapt her speech to that audience using whatever arrangement of ideas, style and delivery is most appropriate. Students of Karl Wallace [a famous 20th century speech professor] are reminded that good reason is the very substance of rhetoric.

One of the reasons that rhetoric is never discussed by reporters in terms of its full import is that the field can be quite complicated, and with a historical precedent of the term being used in a negative manner, it is easier for news, particularly television news, to apply the term to describe ineffective communicators and leave it at that. How would we explain to the general public in sixty seconds or less that the politician who says to his opponent, "Bill that's just mere rhetoric," is himself employing a rhetorical strategy?

Perhaps we could explain it in this way. Rhetoric should be thought of as a protocol--a term familiar in medicine and the military. Were a patient to arrive at a hospital emergency room with an injured leg, the staff would react in a somewhat predictable manner. Questions would be asked to determine the how's and why's of the injury, the hand and eyes of a trained medical professional would examine the limb and if so only then would the leg be X-rayed. When the X-ray was interpreted the leg may or may not be set. Of one thing we can be certain, at any responsible hospital that leg would not be set willy-nilly into a cast without the proper questions being asked or the appropriate personnel having a look into the matter. To rush headlong into a procedure without the proper analysis would violate hospital protocol, that is an established system for behaving in a given situation. A system arrived at through the methodical study of situations that arise, the variables associated with them, the available choices, and the judgment of knowledgeable researchers and practitioners of the field as to what practice might best be employed.

To use the term rhetoric is also to imply the existence of systems or protocols associated with acts of human communication. Rhetoric may be employed to explain a particular response to a situation or to prescribe a response. Choosing one system over another doesn't necessarily guarantee success, but the goal of any good practitioner, pediatrician or rhetorician, is to come as close to success as the particular circumstances might allow and to adhere to the code of ethics that govern his or her practice.

Malpractice can be found in any field, but while a snake oil salesman might profess to be a doctor and sell something that purports to be medicine--we do not judge an entire profession by that person's delusional behavior. It would be nice if the news media would make a more conscientious effort to accord this same courtesy to the professional researchers and practitioners of rhetoric who work in this country and who occasionally have dinner while watching the evening news.

Discussion Questions

1. Before entering this course, what was your definition of "rhetoric"? Or had you ever heard the term?

2. How does Smith (and Aristotle) define rhetoric?

3. How, according to Smith, is rhetoric like medicine?

4. Give examples of public speakers who "practice" rhetoric in ways that heal societal ills?

5. Identify instances of public speakers who should be accused of "rhetorical malpractice."

Activity 1.4: Communication Style (for use with page 12 in the text)

Work in a small group to create a hypothetical culture that contrasts in core ways from ours. (This activity is designed to help you understand how a culture's core beliefs and values affect its public speaking practices.) Create some core beliefs, underlying values, and so on. Then predict forms of public speaking that might exist within the society.

For instance, what might public speaking be like if a group--

- believes that only adult females over the age of 50 are wise enough to speak?
- believes that individuals are not wise enough to make laws; only the ruling elite (women) have any say in policy decisions?
- values conformity and harmony above all else?
- does not feel negative about using physical force to make people conform?
- has no electronic technology, but has print sources?

Core cultural beliefs:

1. about age

2. about roles of men and women

3. other core beliefs

Core values: (for example: honesty, efficiency, peace, honor, duty, self-control, freedom)

1.

2.

3.

Positive attitudes toward

1.

2.

Negative attitudes toward

1.

2.

Degree of expressiveness:

Highly expressive I----------------I-----------------I-----------------I-----------------I--------------I Non-expressive

Given these factors -- Who speaks?

Who is silenced?

Create a story showing how public speakers in this society affect their culture. (See text page 14.)

Before You Take the Exam

To test your knowledge and comprehension of chapter concepts, review the chapter, be able to define key terms, and answer these review questions. (Follow links to the Jaffe text on the Communication Café web site http://communication.wadsworth.com for an interactive list of key terms.)

1. Give three reasons why the study of public speaking is beneficial to most people.
2. Tell who is most likely to suffer from PSA.
3. Identify three elements of communication competence.
4. Explain why a cultural perspective is important.
5. List four types of core cultural resources.
6. Identify ways that people communicate in oral, literate, and electronic cultures.
7. Describe three ways cultures provide expectations about speaking and listening.
8. Identify five elements of the communication style that's most typically used in the U. S.
9. Describe five ways that public speakers influence culture.
10. Draw and label the elements of the transactional model of communication.

Sample questions:

1. You can't hear the speaker because she has laryngitis. In the communication model, this would be depicted as noise. (16)
   - ❍ True
   - ❍ False.
2. About 90% of eighteen- to twenty-four-year-olds feel nervous about public speaking. (5)
   - ❍ True
   - ❍ False.
3. People who grow up in southern regions tend to be more expressive than northerners are. (12)
   - ❍ True
   - ❍ False.
4. Being bicultural is the same as being co-cultural. (8, 13)
   - ❍ True
   - ❍ False.
5. When an imam tells his listeners to continue their charitable works, he is speaking to transform their behaviors. (14)
   - ❍ True
   - ❍ False.

6. Which is NOT an element of communication competence? (5)
   - Knowing how to communicate
   - Feeling confident in the situation
   - Wanting to communicate effectively
   - Giving the message in an understandable manner

7. The oldest book in existence comes from ________ and explains ____________. (8)
   - Egypt . . . how to speak and listen effectively
   - Greece . . . how to use rhetoric effectively
   - Africa . . . how to communicate expressively
   - China . . . how to debate in the Confucian manner
   - Nigeria . . . how women and men should speak

8. Animal rights activists argue that students should stop drinking milk. They are speaking to ______ culture. (14)
   - transmit
   - reinforce
   - restore
   - transform

9. You're listening to a message in which a speaker says, "Voting is stupid." However, because of her tone of voice and other positive things she is saying about voting, you interpret that particular phrase as sarcasm. You are illustrating this part of the communication model. (15)
   - encoding the message
   - channeling the message
   - decoding the message
   - providing feedback
   - coping with noise

10. Many in the U.S. evaluate the First Amendment positively and regulation of speech negatively; these evaluations are part of their core cultural resources known as ____ (9-10)
    - beliefs
    - values
    - attitudes
    - behaviors

Answers to Sample Questions

1. True
2. False
3. True
4. False
5. False
6. Feeling confident in the situation
7. Egypt...how to speak and listen effectively
8. transform
9. decoding the message
10. attitudes

CHAPTER 2: GIVING YOUR FIRST SPEECH: DEVELOPING CONFIDENCE

Activity 2.1: Setting Personal Goals

- What public speaking experiences have you had?
- How well did you do?
- How do you know?
- How did your listeners respond to your speech(es)?

In Activity 1:1, you were asked to identify skills you already have. This chapter provides more details about specific skills. Use Exercise #2 located on pages 33-34 in the text to evaluate your abilities as a public speaker.

- What specific skills have you developed in the canons of invention, disposition, style, memory, and delivery?
- What specific skills do you want to develop or improve?

Set your personal goals for the class. That is, describe exactly what you want to be able to do more effectively as a result of taking this course.

Take the self-test found in Stop and Check: Assess Your Public Speaking Anxiety, located on text page 22. Use the results along with other guidelines in the chapter to create specific strategies you can use to meet the goals you identified above.

Activity 2.2: Rethinking the Canons (pp. 23-29 in the text)

The Romans, not surprisingly, labeled the canons of rhetoric by using Latin words: *inventio, dispositio, elocutio, pronountio,* and *memoria.* In English, we call them invention, disposition or arrangement, style, delivery, and memory. However, the dawn of a new century may be a good time to ask if we should rethink principles of message-making in a print-electronic world.

Take, for example, a high tech movie such as *The Matrix* or *The Lost World.* These films allow the filmmakers, who are prominent cultural storyteller, to produce purposive messages, using all the resources available to them within this culture. Consequently, these movies are rhetorical works created by the use of certain principles or standards.

Work with a group of your classmates to correlate the canons of rhetoric to a movie of your choice. Remember, a canon is defined as *the rules and principles for a specific aspect of message making.* Your task is to describe some principles filmmakers use to create their messages. I'll get you started then use your imagination to see if the principles of rhetoric, identified by the Romans (and Greeks) have relevance for the message production found in today's high-tech movies.

Invention -- What research do the filmmakers or their teams do? What materials are available for their use? What purposes does the film have? What is its central idea? How does the filmmaker support the main ideas?

Disposition -- Organizational pattern? Camera techniques used as transitions? Use of cuts, splices and other editing techniques?

Style -- Language choices? When and where do images replace language?

Delivery -- Machines needed to present the movie? Actors' speaking techniques? Voiceovers?

Memory -- Recording devices? Cue cards for actors?

Activity 2.3: Interview a Public Speaker

Ask someone who regularly speaks in public how she or he prepares for a speech. Examples include business people, trainers, teachers or professors, members of the clergy, police and fire spokespersons. Bring your findings to class and share them with fellow students.

Follow the principles for interviewing described on text page 26, and ask some or all of the following questions:

How do you choose your topic(s)?

What adaptations do you make for different audiences and situations?

How do you go about gathering information for your talks?

How do you generally organize your materials?

What principles for rehearsal have you found most helpful?

Have you ever been nervous about delivering a speech?

If not, why not?

If so, why? And what did you do to overcome your nervousness?

How has public speaking enhanced your career?

What do you see as the value of taking a public speaking course?

Before You Take the Exam

To test your knowledge and comprehension of concepts in chapter 2, review the chapter, be able to define key terms, and answer these review questions. Go to http://communication.wadsworth.com/jaffe for an interactive list of key terms.

1. Tell why learning speechmaking skills can help reduce PSA.
2. List the five canons of speaking and briefly describe what principles you'll find in each.
3. Describe ways your classroom develops features of a culture.
4. List five considerations you make when you choose your topic.
5. Identify three general purposes of speechmaking.
6. Describe how speeches in the U. S. are typically organized.
7. Tell some principles for choosing language for your classroom speeches.
8. List and explain four types of speech delivery.
9. Describe physiological anxiety and explain strategies for dealing with it.
10. Describe psychological anxiety and explain three ways to deal with it.

Sample questions:

1. One study found that learning the process of speech preparation helped demystify speechmaking for very anxious students. (22)
   - ❍ True
   - ❍ False.
2. The canon of invention contains principles for organizing your speeches. (23)
   - ❍ True
   - ❍ False.
3. The canon of style deals with language choices. (23)
   - ❍ True
   - ❍ False.
4. Connectives are words, phrases, and sentences you use to link your ideas. (28)
   - ❍ True
   - ❍ False.
5. The fight-or-flight mechanism is a psychological response to apprehension. (30)
   - ❍ True
   - ❍ False.

6. Another name for the canon of disposition is _______ . (27)
   - ❍ arrangement.
   - ❍ language.
   - ❍ memory.
   - ❍ delivery.

7. When you want your audience to learn something your general purpose is ______. (25)
   - ❍ to inform
   - ❍ to persuade
   - ❍ to influence
   - ❍ to entertain
   - ❍ to convince

8. Which is NOT a general principle for using language in public speeches? (28)
   - ❍ Adapt to audiences on the basis of occupation and age.
   - ❍ Talk like you normally talk so that the audience can get to know the real you.
   - ❍ Avoid demeaning language.
   - ❍ Minimize the use of slang words.

9. I'm awful! They'll think I'm dumb. I can't do this...all these are examples of _____ . (31)
   - ❍ physiological anxiety.
   - ❍ the fight-or-flight mechanism.
   - ❍ internal monologue.
   - ❍ cognitive modification
   - ❍ visualization.

10. Increased heart rate, butterflies, an adrenaline rush--all these are symptoms of ____ . (30)
    - ❍ psychological anxiety.
    - ❍ the fight-or-flight mechanism.
    - ❍ rehearsal anxiety.
    - ❍ cognitive modification.
    - ❍ visualization.

Answers to Sample Questions

1. True
2. False
3. True
4. True
5. False
6. arrangement.
7. to inform.
8. Talk like you normally talk so that the audience can get to know the real you.
9. internal monologue
10. the fight-or-flight mechanism.

CHAPTER 3: ETHICS AND DIVERSITY

Activity 3.1: Explore Your Personal Values (use with pp.39-41 in the text)

Value clashes between individuals and groups often seem irreconcilable. Milton Rokeach identified two basic types of values: instrumental and terminal. Instrumental values are behaviors we consider impor-tant as "means' or instruments to reach a good and worthwhile society. Some are moral values by which we relate to others; others are competence values related to our individual personalities. Terminal values are the goals or ideals that are important "ends" in society. Some have a social focus; others have a personal focus.

Many scholars have made lists of "American" values. The following combined list draws from several sources. Select five values that are personally very significant; then select five you consider least important. In small groups, discuss your choices and the questions that follow the lists.

___ ambition	___ politeness	___ tolerance
___ honesty	___ individuality	___ equality
___ freedom	___ hard work	___ goal achievement
___ optimism	___ success	___ efficiency
___ cleanliness	___ patriotism	___ helping others
___ orderliness	___ wisdom	___ change, progress
___ courage	___ forgiveness	___ a happy family
___ creativity	___ self-control	___ self-reliance
___ dependability	___ friendship	___ world peace
___ prosperity	___ happiness	___ inner peace
___ pleasure	___ self-esteem	___ an exciting life

Discussion Questions:

Which of these values meet the definition of "moral," given above?

Which make you more competent?

Which are social? (Hint: they're paid for with tax money)

Which make you a better person?

How did you learn your personal values?

When you have internal value clashes, what do you tend to do? (For instance, I value both creativity and orderliness, but sometimes it's difficult to have both at once.)

Have you ever participated in a protest of some sort? If so, what were you supporting? What deeply held value made you willing to protest?

Activity 3.2: Explore Your Responses to Diversity (refer to text pp.39-41)

Figure 3.1 (p. 39) shows levels of diversity ranging from minimal to maximum. Think about your campus and make minimum-maximum scale related to campus or community differences. Then assess your own response to each. These differences can be in beliefs (religion, politics, etc.), attitudes (the environment, patriotic symbols, etc.), values (see the list in Activity 3.1), or behavior (lifestyle, noise levels, etc.)

You might:
Resist (attack, agitate against, actively persecute, ignore, discount, taunt or ridicule)
Assimilate (reject, change, surrender your previously held positions)
Accommodate (listen with an open-mind, acknowledge differences but learn about them, accept diversity, work with others on common goals)

Differences on Campus **My Responses to These Differences**

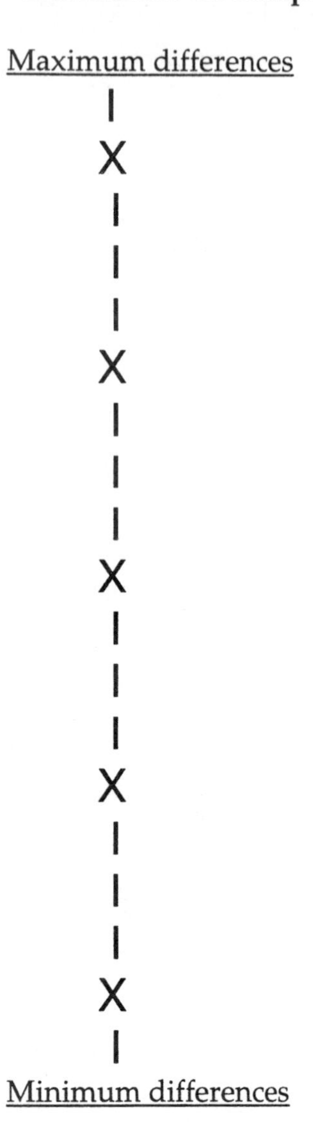

Activity 3.3: Ethical Listening (refer to pp.46-48 in the text)

Read the information about breast cancer statistics as found in Stop and Check: Would You Use Questionable Statistics? (p. 50) Then, listen to impromptu speech #3, "Wear a Ribbon," found on *Student Speeches Video: For Critique and Analysis, Volume I* (available from Wadsworth).

Let's say you are a member of the live audience for this speech, and you feel uneasy that the speaker is passing along information that you know to be faulty or misleading. Your mom or other female relative is with you and she becomes very concerned about her health. What might you say to your relative?

____

____

____

A question and answer period follows the speech; what questions might you ask that allow the speaker to save face but help the audience understand that the statistics are exaggerated?

____

____

____

A second scenario: Instead of a question and answer period, you are asked to give written feedback to the speaker. Write three or four sentence evaluating her entire speech.

____

____

____

____

Compare and contrast the responses you would make to her in a public question and answer period with those you'd make in a private, written form. How are they alike? How are they different? Why is this so?

____

____

____

____

Activity 3.4: Ethical Research and Speaking (for use with pp. 48-50 in the text)

Because public speaking influences the ideas and the behaviors of others, it is important to listen and speak honestly. Occasionally students cross ethical boundaries--both unintentionally and intentionally.

Below are some examples of actual student behaviors--some of which are unethical. (The names, of course, are changed.) Match each example in the box below to one of the following categories:

A. plagiarism
B. fabrication
C. assisting in dishonesty (one person helps another cheat).
D. This behavior is ethically OK.

___ 1. Jim and Joe worked together on a speech; each gave the speech, representing it as his own work.

___ 2. Annika borrowed an outline from Johanna intending to use it as a model for her own. Since it was the night before the speech, and time ran out, Annika just copied the speech and gave it as her own.

___ 3. Johanna loaned her speech outline to Annika, believing that Annika would use it as a model for her own outline. She thought that Annika's topic was entirely different.

___ 4. Carlotta wrote a speech for her best friend.

___ 5. Jeb used a speech from a file in his dorm. He changed a few words, eliminated one main point, and rephrased one section entirely. But he submitted someone else's ideas, general organizational pattern, and supporting materials without doing his own research.

___ 6. Liana listed cited a *Time* magazine article which her instructor happened to have read. The information in the article did not match the content Liana said she'd found in it.

___ 7. Two students gave speeches on the same topic, which were quite different, as would be expected. However, both contained the exact wording on a point or two. Both used one source in common. They both copied an example verbatim from that source. (Neither used quotation marks to indicate it was a direct quotation; neither cited the source.)

___ 8. Erin made up some statistics and cited *Newsweek* as her source.

___ 9. Magdalena gave her outline to her desperate friend who promised never to procrastinate so much again.

___ 10. Greg and Moishe gave speeches on the same topic. Some of their material overlapped, but they did independent research and cited their sources.

What U.S. beliefs and values lead to the emphasis on "doing your own work" in U.S. colleges?

What happens at your school when people are caught cheating?

How might the emphasis on academic honesty change—or be the same--in the year 2050?

Before You Take the Exam

To test your knowledge and comprehension of concepts in chapter 3, review the chapter, be able to define key terms, and answer these review questions. Go to http://communication.wadsworth.com/jaffe for an interactive list of key terms.

1. Explain the maximum-minimum scale that illustrates the range of differences between individuals and groups.
2. Identify and give examples of ways people resist diversity.
3. Identify and give examples of ways people assimilate diverse beliefs and practices.
4. Explain, using examples, the how people can accommodate divergent perspectives.
5. What is the dialogical theory of communication?
6. Compare dialogue and monologue.
7. Give an example of a monological public speaker.
8. Explain the three conditions necessary for dialogue.
9. List characteristics of a dialogical attitude.
10. Identify and explain three guidelines contained in a democratic ethic.
11. Summarize the responsibilities of ethical listeners.
12. Define and give examples of plagiarism and fabrication.

Sample questions:

1. You regularly face ethical communication choices. (38)
   - o True
   - o False.
2. Disputes at the lower end of the maximum-minimum diversity range are rarely divisive. (39)
   - o True
   - o False.
3. The phrase *vir bonum, dicendi peritus* is a Latin phrase that encourages people to listen ethically. (41)
   - o True
   - o False.
4. *Respons*-ibility describes the assimilation response to diversity. (43)
   - o True
   - o False.

5. The host of a political talk show who passes along unsubstantiated rumors in his commentary may be perpetuating a falsehood. (50)
    - o True
    - o False.

6. Joining a protest march against a proposed dam on a river near your campus is an example of the _______ response to diversity. (39)
    - o resisting
    - o accommodation
    - o multivocal
    - o assimilating

7. The ______ theory of communication is formulated around the belief that our earliest conversations form the basis for all other communication. (41-42)
    - o conversational
    - o monological
    - o dialogical
    - o ethical
    - o democratic

8. Which is NOT a required condition for dialogue? (43)
    - o Empathy
    - o Equality
    - o Expressiveness
    - o Examination

9. An example of civility is _______ . (45)
    - o drive-by-debaters.
    - o The commencement speaker's hecklers.
    - o the homosexuals and the Baptists.
    - o Jerry Springer's guests.

10. Ethical listeners ____. (46-47)
    - o give all opinions the right to be heard without comment.
    - o sometimes show disrespect for a speaker who is obviously monological.
    - o listen only to the side of the argument that they already agree with.
    - o try not to distract other listeners.

Answers to Sample Questions

1. true
2. false
3. false
4. false
5. true
6. resisting
7. dialogical
8. Expressiveness
9. the homosexuals and the Baptists.
10. try not to distract other listeners.

CHAPTER 4: EFFECTIVE LISTENING

Activity 4.1: Listening Self-Evaluation: Before, During, and After a Speech

Listen to a videotaped student speech or use this form to evaluate your listening effectiveness to a classroom speaker.

Topic___________________________________

Before the Speech: assess your attitude toward the topic

I know a lot about this topic already.

I-------------------I-------------------I---------------------I-----------------I

Strongly Agree (SA)	Agree (A)	No Opinion (N)	Disagree (D)	Strongly Disagree (SD)

This topic interests me.

I-----------------I----------------I---------------I-----------------I

SA	A	N	D	SD

This topic is significant to my personal life.

I-----------------I----------------I---------------I-----------------I

SA	A	N	D	SD

Given my attitude toward this topic, how would I normally listen? What should I do to listen most effectively?

During the Speech: listen to understand

I have these questions: (Jot down open, closed, or clarification questions, requests for specific information or requests for elaboration).

After the Speech: evaluate your listening effectiveness

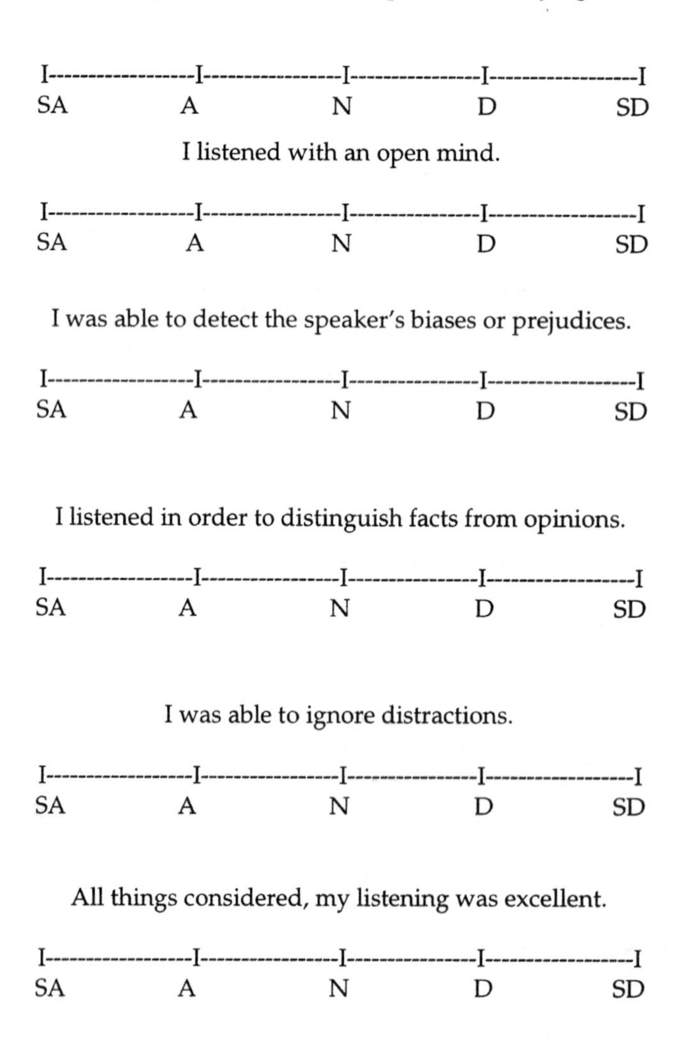

I comprehended what the speaker was saying.

I-----------------I----------------I---------------I-----------------I
SA A N D SD

I listened with an open mind.

I-----------------I----------------I---------------I-----------------I
SA A N D SD

I was able to detect the speaker's biases or prejudices.

I-----------------I----------------I---------------I-----------------I
SA A N D SD

I listened in order to distinguish facts from opinions.

I-----------------I----------------I---------------I-----------------I
SA A N D SD

I was able to ignore distractions.

I-----------------I----------------I---------------I-----------------I
SA A N D SD

All things considered, my listening was excellent.

I-----------------I----------------I---------------I-----------------I
SA A N D SD

My listening was effective in these areas:

I need to improve in these areas:

Activity 4.2: LISTENING SCHEMAS

Schemas are your mental blueprints, plans, or models that help you organize the information you see and hear. Identify your schemas for the following types of speeches or speech acts. In the space provided, list the elements that are typical of the speech or speech act and the organizational pattern these speeches normally use.

For example: **Jokes**

What's included? What's essential? Jokes almost always contain a punch line. Obviously, they should be funny, with an element of the unexpected.

How is the joke typically organized? They often begin with "Did you hear the one about . . . ?" and they end with the punch line.

Funeral eulogies

What's included? What's essential?

How is the eulogy typically organized?

Announcements

What's included? What's essential?

How is the announcement typically organized?

Lectures

What's included? What's essential?

How is the lecture typically organized?

Explain the value of schemas in aiding your listening comprehension. *(For example, when you hear the words, "Did you hear the one about . . . ?" you know that what follows should not be taken literally and you should listen for something funny.)*

Activity 4.3: CASE STUDIES: Student Listeners Confess

If you were a "listening consultant" and these students described their listening habits, how would you diagnose their strengths and weaknesses? What advice would you give them to improve their listening skills?

Student #1: David My listening problems include any and all of the following:
- Interest. I often zone out because of complete lack of interest in the topic.
- How much sleep I've had recently.
- Whether I know I will be responsible for the material or not.
- Other activity around me is distracting. I often don't concentrate because I am still trying to keep track of what's going on around me.
- I don't listen to monotone or boring speakers.

Student #2: Heidi My listening problems include:
- disinterest (My mind wanders and I think, organize, plan parts of my stressful life!)
- busy (no time to listen)
- can't audibly hear them
- misunderstand their meaning—language or vocabulary barrier
- If I get a different meaning than what the speaker intends, my listening and their speaking has glitches.

Activity 4.4: SPEECH CRITIQUE GUIDELINES

Evaluate your classmates' speeches, using the five canons of rhetoric as a guide. Consider these elements of the speech.

In the Canon of Invention

- Topic (appropriate? a need to address this topic?)
- Evidence of research (sources cited? credible sources? major points supported with credible data?)
- Sensitivity to audience (meets their needs? deals with possible objections? respectful? etc.)
- "Good reasons" given for major ideas? (reasoning sound? emotional proofs used well? credible speaker?)

In the Canon of Disposition or Organization

- Introduction (all the parts included? is the intro effective?)
- Body (organizational pattern clear? effectively organized? connectives?)
- Conclusion (all parts here? effective?)

In the Canon of Style

- Clear ideas (avoids or defines jargon?)
- Connotative words (effectively used?)
- Avoids demeaning terminology
- Concise
- Interesting (metaphors? repetition? vivid words? etc.)

In the Canon of Memory

- Knew major ideas
- Few references to notes

In the Canon of Delivery

- Eye contact (inclusive?)
- Appearance (appropriate grooming? clothing? accessories?)
- Voice (effective vocal variety? use of pauses? rate? volume?)
- Time (within limits?)

Especially Effective:

Suggestions for Improvement:

SAMPLE STATEMENTS FOR A CRITIQUE

Topic: Coffee **Informative Purpose**

Invention

- *Well chosen topic! I thought I knew about coffee!*
- *Good adaptation to non-coffee drinkers--a major industry with more workers than any other.*
- *Great facts--from the discovery in Ethiopia, the spread through Africa and into the Muslim culture, then throughout the world. Citing sources = good.*
- *Visuals used well. Thanks for the sample!*
- *Kept my interest. Beethoven really counted out 60 beans/cup?!*

Organization

- *Intro: What's your link to the subject?*
- *Basically topical with chronological sub-point.*
- *Points = easy to distinguish--your preview helped us.*
- *Some repetition in the conclusion--summary = very detailed.*

Style

- *Watch "me and my family." It's "my family and I."*
- *I liked the vivid descriptions of coffee plants and beans.*

Memory

- *Close tie to notes in the intro. Better as you went along.*

Delivery

- *Eye contact sometimes to the instructor, but generally good.*
- *Your gestures = illustrators*
- *Fast in places--especially at the beginning*

Especially Effective:

Keep selecting interesting topics and continue to do the kind of research that adds to our understanding.

Suggestions for improvement:

Look again at your introduction and conclusion to make sure you link yourself to the topic and review only briefly.

Before You Take the Exam

To test your knowledge and comprehension of concepts in chapter 4, review the chapter, be able to define key terms, and answer these review questions. Go to http://communication.wadsworth.com/jaffe for an interactive list of key terms.

1. Compare and contrast the amount of time people spend reading, writing, listening, and speaking.
2. Describe three ways listening skills are valuable.
3. Explain two linguistic barriers to good listening.
4. What cultural barriers can hinder listening?
5. Explain how psychological factors can hinder effective listening.
6. Draw and explain a diagram showing four common thought patterns associated with listening.
7. Explain how listening schema can help you listen better.
8. Identify listening expectations in at least five cultural groups.
9. List four ways to improve comprehensive listening.
10. Explain how you can improve critical listening skills.
11. Describe how posture, distance, and movements can make communication more dialogical.
12. Define and give examples of the following: loaded questions, closed questions, open questions, clarification questions, requests for elaboration, comments, saving face.

Sample questions:

1. Most college students read and write more than they listen. (56)
   - o True
   - o False.
2. Accents and dialects are language differences that can hinder listening. 57-58)
   - o True
   - o False.
3. Going to class when you have the flu is a psychological factor that can hinder listening. (59)
   - o True
   - o False.
4. Another term for the speech-thought differential is "leftover thinking space." (59)
   - o True
   - o False.

5. You use critical listening mainly when you are trying to understand a speech. (63)
   - o True
   - o False.

6. If you were speaking to German students, you'd be more successful if you _____. (63)
   - o tell a lot of personal stories to relate to the audience.
   - o are very organized and precise.
   - o expect them to use the "call and response" pattern.
   - o give a long message, full of complex and challenging information they can think over.

7. Which is NOT a way to improve your comprehension of an informative speech? (63)
   - o Prepare in advance.
   - o Plan strategies to direct your attention to specific elements of the speech.
   - o Use small departures to link the material to your personal experiences.
   - o Try to find flaws in the speech.
   - o Pay attention to words and phrases that identify main ideas and link ideas together.

8. "Can you tell me more strategies I can use to rehearse for a speech?" is an example of a(n) ___(66)
   - o closed question.
   - o open question.
   - o comment on the speech content.
   - o loaded question.
   - o request for elaboration.

9. Which is NOT a cultural allusion? (58)
   - o My grandmother is warmhearted.
   - o Adherents to Judiasm do not eat ham.
   - o Marie Antoinette went to the guillotine.
   - o The Moors greatly influenced Spanish architecture.
   - o Ibn Sina taught that things have "necessary being" and "contingent being."

10. The average listener recalls only about ____ of what she hears. (56)
    - o 75%-80%
    - o 1/3
    - o 1/2
    - o 25%
    - o 10%

Answers to Sample Questions

1. False
2. True
3. False
4. True
5. False
6. are very organized and precise.
7. Try to find flaws in the speech.
8. a request for elaboration.
9. My grandmother is warmhearted.
10. 25%

CHAPTER 5: AUDIENCE ANALYSIS

Activity 5.1: Audience Motivations Worksheet

Identify a specific occupation that interests you: ______________________________

List opportunities (if any) that a person in that occupation might have to address an audience with each of the following motivations:

Pedestrian

Passive

Selected

Concerted

Organized

Absent

Which type(s) of audience(s) will probably be most common for this profession? (Give specific examples.) Why?

Which type(s) of audience(s) will be least common? Why?

Activity 5.2: Case Study: Time Violations

Professor Brain consistently violates time norms. Sometimes she continues her lecture up to six minutes after the class is scheduled to end. At other times, she's late to class then she shuffles papers and talks to students so that she doesn't actually start until about twenty minutes into the class period. On occasion, she skips class entirely--with no note on the classroom door and no explanation.

1. Would you stay when Prof Brain is late? Why or why not? How often would you stay? How long? How would you feel?

2. How would you signal Professor Brain that her time is up and she should quit talking so that you can get to your next class which is across campus?

3. What's your response if you come to class (it's your only class that day, and you made a real effort to get there) and there's no Brain and no message?

4. Would it make a difference if you found out later that she had a doctor's appointment that she'd scheduled two weeks ago? What if she had an emergency flat tire on the way to work? Would it make a difference if it were a sunny day, and some students saw her out for a drive in the country?

5. Are any of her behaviors grounds for some kind of administrative discipline? If so, what? Why?

6. What end-of-the-course evaluation would you give her?

7. What can you learn from this that applies to time limits on classroom speeches? To speaking on your scheduled day? To expectations in your future occupation?

Activity 5.3: Assess the Speaker's Credibility

Martin Sheen, the actor who plays the president on NBC television's "*West Wing*," regularly speaks out regarding political issues. Before the war with Iraq, he predicted that 500,000 people would be killed.

If you were bored one night and turned on the TV where you saw Mr. Sheen arguing this way, would you consider him a credible speaker? What prior or extrinsic credibility would you say he had regarding the following:

Political power in general?

Intelligence information regarding Iraq?

Information about the U.S. military?

Sheen made his prediction in February 2003. How do was his terminal credibility affected by the international events that followed?

.....

Rock star **Bono** (lead singer for the Irish band *U2*) has had audiences with Presidents Bush and Clinton and with Pope John Paul II, whose support he enlisted in his quest for Third World debt relief. What credibility can a rock star have regarding international policy questions?

When he meets with the presidents and the Pope what prior credibility does he bring?

Do his experiences as an Irishman contribute to his credibility? If so, how?

How can he demonstrate credibility as he speaks out for this cause?

After his audiences with these world leaders, how might they assess his terminal credibility?

What other celebrities have influenced public policy? Why? What was their credibility on their subjects?

Before You Take the Exam

To test your knowledge and comprehension of concepts in chapter 5, review the chapter, be able to define key terms, and answer these review questions. Go to http://communication.wadsworth.com/jaffe for an interactive list of key terms.

1. Identify six types of audience motivation, and explain the challenges a speaker faces with each audience.

2. Give at least two examples showing how the salience of a demographic feature can vary from speech situation to situation.

3. Distinguish between ethnicity and race.

4. Differentiate between gender, marital status, and sexual expression, and give examples of sexist assumptions.

5. Identify four major age categories, and list characteristics that are typical of people in each.

6. Describe ways that religion, group affiliation, occupation or socioeconomic status, and region can each influence an audience.

7. Explain the following elements of a psychological audience profile: beliefs, attitudes, values.

8. Give examples of ways that situational factors of time and the environment affect an audience.

9. Show how prior, demonstrated, and terminal credibility work together to give an audience confidence in a speaker.

Sample test questions:

1. Audiences in the United States take a very relaxed attitude toward speakers and time constraints. (82)
   - ❍ True
   - ❍ False.

2. Racial categories are distinct from one another. (74)
   - ❍ True
   - ❍ False.

3. Age has a major influence on listeners' motivations and concerns. (75-76)
   - ❍ True
   - ❍ False.

4. The journalist and columnist William Raspberry is asked to speak at your school on some aspect of news reporting; he brings with him prior credibility. (83-84)
   - ❍ True
   - ❍ False.

5. Felicia has good feelings about tattooing; in short, she has a positive attitude toward it. (79)
   - ❍ True
   - ❍ False.

6. Juan is a gay Latino, but his ethnic or sexual identity is not particularly _______ in his chemistry class; what matters more is his focus on his future occupation. (74)
   - ❍ racist
   - ❍ salient
   - ❍ demographic
   - ❍ sexist

7. A(n) ____ audience made up of passersby is more challenging to attract than is a(n) _____ audience who really want to hear a specific speaker. (73)
   - ❍ hostile . . . passive
   - ❍ passive . . . concerted
   - ❍ pedestrian . . . selected
   - ❍ pedestrian . . . passive
   - ❍ hostile . . . organized

8. Gerard talked about the Muslim month of Ramadan, assuming that everyone knew what it was. His mistake was that he ___________. (74)
   - ❍ failed to take into account audience motivations.
   - ❍ didn't do adequate demographic audience analysis.
   - ❍ should have taken a psychological profile of his audience's attitude toward Islam.
   - ❍ failed to consider that he lacked prior credibility on the subject.

9. The _____ generation tends to be individualistic and "me"-centered; ________ are sometimes called the I-generation (I = Internet). (75-76)
   - ❍ mature . . . baby boomers
   - ❍ baby boomer . . . Generation Xers
   - ❍ X . . . the millenium generation
   - ❍ Baby boomer . . . millenium generation
   - ❍ Mature . . . Generation Xers

10. Ronnie always kept in mind that her listeners had just come from lunch; she was aware of ___ factors. (81-82)
    - ❍ motivational
    - ❍ demographic
    - ❍ situational
    - ❍ psychological

Answers to Sample Questions

1. False
2. False
3. True
4. True
5. True
6. salient
7. pedestrian . . . selected
8. he didn't do adequate demographic audience analysis .
9. baby boomer . . . millenium generation
10. situational

CHAPTER 6: SELECTING YOUR TOPIC AND PURPOSE

Activity 6.1: Topic Questionnaire

Early in the term identify interesting topics so that you can be alert for material throughout the term. Use the following questions to guide you:

People

traits you consider admirable?

people who embody these traits?

other interesting people?

Concepts

enjoyable courses?

interesting concepts?

Personal Experiences

hobbies or recreational pursuits?

job related experiences?

health related experiences?

Current Issues

___ Crime (prevention, punishment, prisoner lawsuits, the drug war)
___ Civil rights (of women and minorities, international rights)
___ Weapons (metal detectors, nuclear, historical weapons, car bombs)
___ Personal (health, self-defense, job security, time management)
___ Privacy issues (Internet privacy, the Patriot Act, caller ID, lifestyle choices)
___ Entertainment (violent video games, sports salaries, cable TV)

International/Cultural Topics

controversial international issues?

interesting facts or traditions from another country?

topics from your ethnic heritage?

culture clashes in the United States?

Create a mind map using one of these general categories as your major theme.

Activity 6.2: Assess the Appropriateness of a Topic

Watch the student speech "Drinking and Driving" (Speech #8, Student Speeches Video: for Critique and Analysis, Vol. I available through Wadsworth).

Outline the speech as you watch, then answer the following:

General Purpose:

Specific Purpose:

Central Idea:

This topic is probably familiar to most of the audience. Assess how well the speaker successfully adapts to his audience's need to know.

Is the topic significant to a college audience? Why or why not?

What do you already know about it? Do you think your knowledge level is typical of college students?

What, if any, new information does the speaker provide? That is, do you learn anything from this presentation?

Does the speaker take a novel approach? If so, how? If not, what should he have done to make the speech more appropriate to this audience?

Look back at the specific purpose you identified above. Did he mainly target a cognitive, affective, or behavioral goal? How well do you think he accomplished his goals?

This is an example of a student giving a speech he did not write. (Producers of the video liked the speech and wanted to show a student giving it; the author of the speech was unavailable, and this speaker adapted and presented it in her place.) How successful is he, in your opinion? Why?

Activity 6.3: Worksheet: Purpose Statements and Central Ideas

Write purpose statements and a central idea for each outline of main points. (See text pages 104-109.)

I. General Purpose:

Specific Purpose:

Central Idea:

Main Points:
- A. Face-lifts are common cosmetic surgeries.
- B. Many people have their noses reconstructed.
- C. Chin augmentation is a type of plastic surgery.

II. General Purpose:

Specific Purpose:

Central Idea:

Main Points:
- A. Healthy blood donors are always needed.
- B. Donating blood requires minimal effort.
- C. Your reward is the knowledge that you helped someone.
- D. Donate today at the on-campus bloodmobile.

III. General Purpose:

Specific Purpose:

Central Idea:

Main Points:
- A. Chinese writing contains pictures of objects.
- B. Some symbols are ideas in picture form.
- C. Some represent abstract ideas
- D. Other words stand for lessons.

IV. General Purpose:

Specific Purpose:

Central Idea:

Main Points:
- A. First, is the transition from drowsiness to sleep.
- B. It's easy to awaken in the next step--light sleep.
- C. The third and fourth stages are called deep sleep.
- D. Vivid dreams occur in REM (rapid eye movement) sleep.

V. General Purpose:

Specific Purpose:

Central Idea:

Main Points:
- A. Some people learn prejudice at home.
- B. Prejudice can result from fear or ignorance.
- C. Some people's prejudices are a reaction to mistreatment.

Activity 6.4: Headings for Outlines and Speeches

On pages 98-99 of the text, you'll find headings for three speeches which are either outlined or written out in the text. Select one topic that interests you and read the entire speech or outline to see how the speaker develops the ideas that she summarizes in her heading. Decide how well the speaker accomplished her stated goals.

- You'll find the "Dolphin Communication" outline in Appendix C.
- "Medical Misinformation on the Internet" is outlined at the end of Chapter 7.
- You can read through the speech on "Sleep Deprivation" (and see a second outline on the same topic) in Appendix C.

Before You Take the Exam

To test your knowledge and comprehension of concepts in chapter 6, review the chapter, be able to define key terms, and answer these review questions. Go to http://communication.wadsworth.com/jaffe for an interactive list of key terms.

1. Discuss ways you can assess your audience's need to know.
2. List sources for topics and give an example of a topic from each source.
3. Explain the importance of connecting the topic to audience interests.
4. Summarize the findings of the study that examined the relationship between empathy and the way diversity is taught in a communication course.
5. Give an example showing how the three general purposes described in the chapter can overlap in a single speech.
6. What three areas of audience response do specific purposes statements generally target?
7. Explain two ways of writing a specific purpose statement.
8. Explain what the central idea is and give other names for it.
9. Identify guidelines for writing a central idea.

Sample questions:

1. Once you write out your central idea, you rarely change it. (98)
   - ❍ True
   - ❍ False.
2. It's generally considered cheating if you do a speech based on research you did for a paper in another course. (92)
   - ❍ True
   - ❍ False.

3. A mind map is one way to narrow your topic effectively. (93-94)
   - ❍ True
   - ❍ False.

4. "To inform my audience about the difference between plagiarism and fabrication" is an example of a central idea. (96)
   - ❍ True
   - ❍ False.

5. You should state your central idea is some form in the speech itself. (99)
   - ❍ True
   - ❍ False.

6. The student who made a peanut butter and jelly sandwich was ineffective because ______. (90)
   - ❍ The audience was too familiar with the topic to be interested.
   - ❍ The speech went only over old material; there was no novelty.
   - ❍ She overestimated what her audience already knew.
   - ❍ She treated a familiar topic in an unfamiliar way.

7. Shaun wants his audience to believe that the earth has been visited by UFOs; his general purpose is ______. (96)
   - ❍ to inform
   - ❍ to persuade
   - ❍ to entertain
   - ❍ to motivate

8. Which is NOT another name for central idea mentioned in the text? (97)
   - ❍ residual message
   - ❍ core idea
   - ❍ subject sentence
   - ❍ summary idea

9. Which is NOT an advantage of choosing a topic from events covered in the media? (92)
   - ❍ They usually address a need in society.
   - ❍ They are significant to many people.
   - ❍ They are automatically relevant to your classroom audience.
   - ❍ Information is generally easy to find.

10. From the research on empathy and diversity in course requirements, you can probably conclude ________. (99)
    - ❍ choosing one communication and diversity topic will probably help you gain a great deal of empathy.
    - ❍ discussing diversity throughout the semester is one way to increase your empathy.
    - ❍ you are likely to gain in empathy, even if you are part of a control group.
    - ❍ you should take an entire course in intercultural communication if you hope to gain empathy.

Answers to Sample Questions

1. False
2. False
3. True
4. False
5. True
6. The speech went only over old material; there was no novelty.
7. to persuade.
8. summary idea
9. They are automatically relevant to your classroom audience.
10. Discussing diversity throughout the semester is one way to increase your empathy.

CHAPTER 7: RESEARCHING YOUR SPEECH IN AN ELECTRONIC CULTURE

Activity 7.1: Library Research

Use the computerized catalog in your library to complete this assignment.

Author Search

Find a book by Deborah Tannen. Write the call letters in this space. ________ Follow this example of source citation.

Author's last name, first initial. middle initial. (date). Title, underlined or italicized, with only the first word, proper nouns, and the first word of the subtitle capitalized. City of publication: Company.

____

____

Subject Search: Eating Disorders

Book. Call letters: ______ Cite correctly, using the pattern for bibliographic citation shown above:

____

____

Magazine or Journal Article. Follow this citation form:

Author(s)' last name, first initial. middle initial. (year, month, day). Title--capitalized as noted above. Magazine title underline or italicized,, volume underlined, page number(s).

____

____

Newspaper Article. Follow this source citation format:

Author(s)' last, first initial. middle initial. (year, month, day). Title. Newspaper title underlined or italicized, edition, p. number(s).

____

____

Electronically Stored Data. Find a television program or movie about anorexia or bulimia.

Last name, first initial. middle initial. (Producer). & Last name, first initial. middle initial. (Director). (date). Title underlined or italicized. [Television program]. Company.

____

____

Reference Section

Go to the reference section of the library and browse through the offerings there. Write the title of two interesting dictionaries you find. [examples: *New Dictionary of American Slang; A Dictionary of Pianists.*]

______________________________ ______________________________

Write three interesting encyclopedia titles. [examples: *The Encyclopedia of Phobias, Fears, and Anxieties. The Encyclopedia of Music in Canada.*]

______________________________ ______________________________

____

Periodicals

Congressional Digest Find this periodical in your library. (If you don't have it, ask your reference librarian if the library carries a similar journal that summarizes both sides of controversial issues.)

Select an issue on a topic that interests you. Skim through the periodical and, in the space below, jot down the features it offers that can help you research current or ongoing issues of national and global importance.)

Activity 7.2: Computer Topic Search

1. Purpose and Scope of Search. Before you sit down at the computer to do a subject search, summarize your topic as completely and concisely as possible. For example: What has been the effect of computers on banking techniques both nationally and internationally?

Now, summarize your own search topic in one or two sentences.

____

____

____

2. Identify Main Concepts. Underline or circle the main concepts in the summary statement you wrote above. For example:

What has been the effect of [computers] on [banking] [techniques] both nationally and internationally?

3. Select Subject Terms. List the terms that describe your main concepts. Ask a Reference Librarian for a guide that will identify appropriate terms for a computer search. For example:

First term(s)	Second term(s)	Third term(s)
computers	banking	techniques
or	or	or
minicomputers	banks	methods
or	or	or
microcomputers	international banking	procedures

Now, enter the subject terms for *your* computer search:

First term(s)	Second Term(s)	Third Term(s)
__________	__________	__________
or	or	or
__________	__________	__________
or	or	or
__________	__________	__________

Proceed by actually conducting your own search.

Adapted from a worksheet prepared by St. John's University librarians.

Activity 7.3: Internet Research

Internet Site #1: Go to the following site on the internet:

http://www.house.gov

What is the overall title of the site? ______________________________

Who sponsors this site? ______________________________

What is the purpose of this site?

When was this site last updated? ________________________________

In the space provided, enter your zip code and find your congressional representative. Go to his or her home page. Read the biographical material provided. Tell two interesting facts you discovered:

Return to www.house.gov. Find and list four items scheduled for this week on the floor of the house:

A.

B.

C.

D.

Follow the link on one of these agenda items and find out the following:

What's the number of the bill? ________________________________

What's the bill about?

What's the status of the bill?

Explore other links on this site and briefly summarize what you did.

How reliable is the information is on this website? Give reasons for your evaluation.

Internet Site #2: Connect to a search engine such as www.google.com or yahoo.com. Search for "mehndi."

What is the location of the site you choose? http:www.______________________

What can you discover about the history of this art form?

What equipment or supplies do you need for this art?

Locate at least four related Web pages and write their URLs here:

1.

2.

3.

4.

Compare and contrast information you find on two different Web pages. How are they alike? How are they different?

Which of these links appeals to you most? Why?

Explore other related sites, and briefly describe what you did.

How reliable is the information you find on various sites? Give reasons for your evaluation.

Before You Take the Exam

To test your knowledge and comprehension of the concepts in Chapter 7, review the chapter, be able to define key terms, and answer these review questions. Go to http://communication.wadsworth.com/jaffe for an interactive list of key terms.

1. List nine guidelines that will help you conduct research more wisely.

2. Distinguish between primary sources and secondary sources and give examples of each in oral, print, and electronic resources.

3. Give six tips for conducting an interview.

4. Describe nine types of library resources you can use for speech materials.

5. Tell how to integrate mass media resources into a research plan.

6. List five characteristics of the Internet.

7. Explain browsers, HTML, URLs, subject directories, and text indexes.

8. Explain factors you must consider in order to evaluate Internet sources critically.

9. Describe three ways to record research information.

10. Be able to cite material from books, newspapers, periodicals, interviews, mass media sources, and the Internet.

Sample Questions

1. You will most likely use oral, print, mass media, and Internet sources in every speech you create. (105)
   - ❍ True
   - ❍ False

2. Identifying the key term for a subject search is an important part of library research. (105)
   - ❍ True
   - ❍ False

3. Tools, jewelry, clothing and other relics or artifacts are secondary sources of information. (106)
   - ❍ True
   - ❍ False

4. It's best not to use your personal experiences in persuasive speeches. (107)
   - ❍ True
   - ❍ False

5. A subject directory is like your telephone's yellow pages. (116)
   - ❍ True
   - ❍ False

6. Which is NOT a characteristic of the Internet? (115)
   - It's democratic.
   - It provides up-to-the-minute information.
   - It costs so much that most poor people have no access to it.
   - It is interactive.

7. When you look at the .edu or .gov or .org of a URL and use it to judge the credibility of an Internet site, you are __________. (117)
   - considering the organization of the material.
   - evaluating the source of the information.
   - examining the content of the information.
   - assessing the accuracy of the site.

8. The advantage information cards have over mind maps or photocopies is _____ . (123)
   - they are most effective for holistic learning styles.
   - they take advantage of the Fair Use provision of the federal Copyright Act.
   - you can more easily use highlighters on them to identify salient information.
   - you can easily arrange and reshuffle your ideas before writing your outline.

9. One advantage of newspapers over television news is they _______. (111)
   - are better for breaking news stories.
   - generally provide more in-depth coverage of issues and events.
   - have human interest stories as well as hard news.
   - have more primary sources than secondary sources.

10. When you want to search the Internet for an exact title such as "My First Lie and How I Got Out of It" you will probably find it more efficiently if you use a _____ . (117)
    - text index.
    - specific URL.
    - subject directory.
    - webliography.

Answer Bank

1. false
2. true
3. false
4. false
5. true
6. It costs so much that most poor people have no access to it.
7. evaluating the source of the information.
8. you can easily arrange and reshuffle your ideas before writing your outline.
9. they generally provide more in-depth coverage of issues and events.
10. a text index.

CHAPTER 8: CHOOSING SUPPORTING MATERIALS

Activity 8.1: Fact-Opinion Worksheet

The following evidence comes from the types of materials students typically use in their speeches. Write "F" beside factual statements and "O" beside statements of opinion. Then discuss your answers with a group of your classmates..

Title IX: Is it fair to men's sports?

Orecklin, M. (2003, March 3). Now she's got game. *Time*, 161(9), accessed 2/25/03 at http://www.time.com/time/magazine/article/0,9171,1101030303-426059,00.html.

___ The pavilion at the University of Connecticut's campus seats 10,000 people; whenever the women's basketball team plays there, the place sells out.

___ The women's Huskies team is more popular than the men's squad.

___ The school probably would not have allotted the funds for a first-rate coach to develop the program if it were not for Title IX funds.

___ Thirty-one years ago when Title IX was written, women needed help to achieve equality in numbers on the playing field.

___ The women Huskies have won 64 games in a row.

___ Marquette University dropped its men's wrestling program, which was mostly funded privately, in order to create parity between the number of sports for women and men.

___ Jessica Gavorin, author of *Tilting the Playing Field*, says Title IX was important when it was legislated, but now it is "being used as a preference, not as a shield against discrimination."

Roadside Memorials

Whitacre, D. (2001, November 8). North Carolina bans roadside memorials. *Knight Ridder/Tribune News Service. Accessed 2/28/03 InfoTrac College Edition.*

___ North Carolina passed a law banning wreaths, crosses, and other roadside memorials put up by grieving families to mark a spot where a loved one died in a traffic accident.

___ Grieving families say they remind them and other drivers of a life needlessly lost.

___ Highway officials urge grieving families to join the Adopt-a-Highway program instead; if they do, officials will put up two signs bearing the loved one's name.

___ ". . . memorials are very important to the family and helps them in the grieving process," said one widow.

___ Mike Owensby lost his daughter Kirsten in a car wreck last summer, but he didn't put up a memorial because he finds them distracting.

___The poignant markers are common along interstate highways and roads.

Activity 8.2: Evaluating Evidence

The following is a speech Chris Russie (Pacific Lutheran University) gave at competitive speech meets throughout the northwest. Read it and identify the types of support he uses then, using the tests in the text, evaluate the effectiveness of his support.

Do you know that with use of modern technology you can be made into a perfect and permanent object of incredible beauty? There is one down side however -- first you have to die.

What am I talking about? you may ask yourself. Well I'll tell you. A new company called LifeGem can take your cremated ashes and make diamonds out of you. Creepy? Perhaps, but before passing judgment, we should examine the company and their diamonds, the process for making these diamonds, and finally the need that such a service fulfills in our society. LifeGem allows people in the search for immortality to find it in some degree, in innovation.

What is LifeGem? LifeGem is a company, but more than that it is a product and an idea, that helps people deal with the loss of the recently departed. According to their website, LifeGem.com, this company was founded after three years of intensive research and development. They produce certified high quality diamonds from the cremated ashes of people -- or their pets.

LifeGem believes that it is important to honor the dead, but that the experience of the survivors is equally important. They hope to be able to provide for families' distinct and individual needs, in producing a memorial to the ones they have lost.

- *Major type of support?*
- *Effectiveness?*

Since the *Chicago Tribune* ran a front page article about LifeGem on August 20th the company's website has received approximately 20,000 hits daily, according to the September 13th *The Vista* Online.

- *Major type of support?*
- *Effectiveness?*

In their product line, LifeGem carries between .25 carat diamonds for about $2,000-- minimum order of two, and 1.3 carat diamonds which are not yet available. Presently the diamonds come in three colors, blue, yellow and red, and in the future they plan to create clear diamonds as well.

- *Major type(s) of support?*
- *Effectiveness?*

In order to assure customers of the quality of their diamonds and to avoid any bias, LifeGem anonymously sent diamonds to be certified for quality by the European Gemological Laboratory before going public. . . . Greg Herro, head of LifeGem Memorials, claims that an August 21 news release by Reuters reported the diamonds are of the same quality "you would find at Tiffany's." The European Gemological Laboratory, according to the August 22nd *Milwaukee Journal Sentinel*, has since been certifying all of LifeGem's diamonds.

- *Major type of support?*
- *Effectiveness?*

The idea for LifeGem started three years ago, according to the August 20th *Chicago Tribune*, when its creator and current chief operating officer, Rusty VandenBiesen, decided that he didn't want his final resting place to be in a cemetery or in an urn left on a fireplace mantle. He didn't know much about biochemistry or synthetic diamonds, but given that the body is in large part carbon, he figured that it should be possible to make diamonds, if he could find some way to extract a person's carbon.

- *Major type of support?*
- *Effectiveness?*

This might lead one to ask, how are LifeGems made? LifeGem clients take a posthumous trip around the world. This trip has five stages, a European lab, a crematorium in Chicago, another lab in Pennsylvania, back to Europe, and finally, home. After several years of trial and error, an American owned lab outside of Munich successfully produced diamonds out of a cadaver, claiming that one body could yield up to 50 stones of varying sizes. That number has now been increased to over 100 stones, according to LifeGem.com. This trip is of course the first and most important step, for with out it the rest of our journey would be impossible.

- *Major type of support?*
- *Effectiveness?*

Just after her death, the client is transported to a cremation facility–let's say in Chicago--that has an arrangement with LifeGem. She is then stored for one or two days according to state law.

After that, she undergoes a special cremation where technicians control oxygen levels in order to minimize the conversion of the carbon into carbon dioxide. Before the incineration has been completed the technicians halt the process long enough to collect the carbon. The cremation process then continues normally according to the *Chicago Tribune*. Afterwards, the remains are removed from the chamber. Any foreign material such as shrapnel or bridgework is removed and typically discarded, according to LifeGem.com.

The remains are then processed to a consistent size and shape and placed in an urn of the family's choosing. If there is no urn, the remains are sent home in a cardboard or plastic container.

According to the *Journal Sentinel*, The carbon powder that was extracted during the cremation process is sent to Pennsylvania where it is heated in a vacuum at 3,000 degrees Celsius or 5,400 degrees Fahrenheit, which turns it into graphite.

This graphite, in turn, is sent to the lab in Germany or to the Technological Institute for Superhard and Novel Carbon Materials near Moscow. There it will be placed around a diamond a few thousandths of a millimeter across to aid the crystallization process. Next, it is subjected to intense heat and pressure, roughly 80 thousand times the atmospheric pressure, replicating the forces involved in making a naturally occurring diamond, according to the September 3rd edition of the *Boston Globe*. This whole process takes about 16 weeks, according to Reuters.

The last and final step of this journey, as I am sure you have all suspected, is returning home. LifeGem will now send the client, in her new diamond form, back home to her family.

- *Major type of support?*
- *Effectiveness?*

What possible function can this procedure serve? Our society has a growing demand for non-traditional funerals. According to *USA Today*, last year 26% of Americans who died were cremated, triple the number from 1973. By the year 2010 The Cremation Association of North America expects that number will jump to nearly 40%.

A primary reason for this change in American behavior is the rising cost of traditional funerals. Embalming and high-end coffins have raised the cost of the average funeral to $6,130. In contrast, cremations can cost less than one thousand dollars according to the National Funeral Directors Association. LifeGem can produce a single, quarter carat diamond for $2,000. Even with the requirement of purchasing at least half a carat of diamonds, there is still a significant price difference.

This behavior is not isolated in America. One of LifeGem's goals is to break into the Japanese market, where, according to the *Chicago Tribune*, the national cremation rate is more than 98%. This is due, in large part, to the exorbitantly high property values.

- *Major type of support?*
- *Effectiveness?*

Another important feature of American society, that such an industry cannot ignore, is the way that people shower their pets with love, attention, and perhaps most importantly for this discussion, money. LifeGem plans to market their services in veterinarians' offices across the U.S. "People would wear a LifeGem to show off the love, light and energy that came from their animals, too," states Herro. The pet market might in fact turn out to be significant, according to the *Boston Globe*. The company has had about 100 inquires from people who were interested in the process for person and more than 100 inquires about using this process to immortalize a pet.

- *Major type of support?*
- *Effectiveness?*

It would seem logical to assume that price is not the only reason for this increase. People want to do something original with themselves, not only in life, but in death as well. This is clearly illustrated in the growing number of new forms of funerals. According to *USA Today*, the remains of Frisbee inventor Ed Headrick are being made into flying discs. Eternal Reefs in Atlanta will mix human ashes and concrete to produce artificial coastal reefs. According to the September 29th *Independent on Sunday* (London), Celestius, Inc. of the U.S. will launch your cremated ashes into space, an option that Gene Rodenberry chose. As you can see people are being encouraged to be creative with their deaths. LifeGem provides another way they can do so.

- *Major type of support?*
- *Effectiveness?*

One of Rusty VandenBiesen's hopes was that people could have something very personal to remember their loved ones with. He thought that urns and cemetery plots fail to inspire memories and discussions about loved ones who have passed away. He didn't like the idea of being forgotten.

- *Major type of support?*
- *Effectiveness?*

So as you can see, you can be made into a perfect and permanent object of incredible beauty. LifeGem uses an extensive process to produces high quality diamonds that do fulfill an actual societal demand. LifeGems provide people with a connection to those who have passed on, and a measure of immortality for those who never want to disappear.

Activity 8.3: Testing Statistics

Read each example then answer the questions that follow.

The Princeton Dental Resource Center provides newsletters for dentists to distribute to patients. One issue contained the startling claim that eating chocolate might aid in keeping plaque bacteria down. Some researchers, studying the relationship between different foods and cavities, found chocolate bars to produce only 72% as many cavities as pure sugar caused. The Princeton group (run by two dentists) failed to report that they received about 90% of their million dollar budget from a candy company.

- *What test(s) for quantification does this study fail to meet?*
- *What additional information would you like to have about the study?*
- *How might the funding source affect the findings?*
- *Does the word "Princeton" in the company's name influence your thinking? (E.g. what if it were the Hoboken Dental Resource Center?)*

On July 8, 2002, a news anchor on KOIN television in Portland, Oregon, introduced a news segment by saying, "You are more likely to die of eating peanut butter than being in a plane crash. So what are your chances of being in a terrorist attack?"

- *What is the average person's chance of dying because of eating peanut butter? (e.g. 1:100,000? I am personally not allergic to peanuts. What would make me die?)*
- *How do you think the anchor got this comparison?*
- *What, specifically, do you know about your chance of being in a plane crash, given this information?*
- *What does this tell you about your chances of being in a terrorist attack?*

In an informative speech about artificial blood, one speaker said that 97% of people would need a blood transfusion during their lifetime, but only 1 in 3 eligible people would donate blood.

- *Does this percentage make sense to you? Have you ever had a blood transfusion? Under what conditions might you need one? Think about all the people you know. How many have had a blood transfusion? Of all the people who've died in your town or city during the past year, what percentage do you think have had a blood transfusion during their lifetimes? Do you think 97% is accurate or overstated? How do you think her sources got this percentage? How might she check this?*
- *Why do you think the speaker used 97% for one statistic 1 in 3 for the other?*
- *The speaker also reported that 302 million transfusions had taken place since the 1930s. How might this fact contribute to the percentage?*
- *Note that the speaker said "1 in 3 eligible donors." What factors might make people ineligible to donate blood? How might you find out what percentage of people are eligible donors?*
- *How might you present the statistics differently to create a different impression?*

Before You Take the Exam

To test your knowledge and comprehension of Chapter 8 concepts, review the chapter, be able to define key terms, and answer these review questions. You can go online to http://communication.wadsworth.com/jaffe for an interactive list of key terms.

1. Explain types of factual material and describe ways to test facts.
2. Describe the advantages of examples and explain how to use examples effectively.
3. Tell three tests for examples.
4. Identify ways to use and test quotations.
5. Explain the benefits and drawbacks of using numerical data in speeches.
6. Distinguish the types of statistics, and give tips for using statistics effectively.
7. Describe both figurative and literal analogies and explain how to test analogies.

Sample Questions

1. Using examples is a good way to help listeners connect with a topic emotionally. (134)
   - ❍ True
   - ❍ False

2. Paraphrasing is generally less effective than quoting a person directly. (138)
   - ❍ True
   - ❍ False

3. Oral traditions are good sources of cultural proverbs. (140)
   - ❍ True
   - ❍ False

4. Rounding off large numbers is more effective than giving a precise count. (141)
   - ❍ True
   - ❍ False

5. In serious speeches speakers rarely use figurative analogies. (146)
   - ❍ True
   - ❍ False

6. "The teacher spent most of his days in drill sergeant mode" is an example of _____. (146)
   - ❍ a hypothetical example.
   - ❍ a verifiable fact.
   - ❍ an analogy.
   - ❍ a paraphrase of a culturally accepted expert's opinion.

7. One advantage of using the median is that it ____________. (143)
   - ❍ eliminates numbers at the extreme ends of the range, thus it is more realistic.
   - ❍ shows the average number in a series of numbers.
   - ❍ is the number that appears most commonly, thus is more realistic.
   - ❍ is more difficult to use in a deceptive manner.

8. Dictionary definitions are a type of ___________. (133)
   - ❍ fact.
   - ❍ example.
   - ❍ culturally accepted quotation.
   - ❍ literal analogy.

9. For your speech on restoring antique cars, you quote a cousin who tinkers with cars on her day off. She is a _____ source. (138)
   - ❍ factual
   - ❍ hypothetical
   - ❍ peer
   - ❍ expert

10. Using examples from her experiences as a nanny gives Sara more competence because ___. (135)
    - ❍ listeners will tend to take her examples as established facts.
    - ❍ she is better able to describe the situation in more vivid detail.
    - ❍ she demonstrates that she has first hand experience.
    - ❍ she can use literal analogies more effectively because she's been a nanny herself.

Answer Bank

1. true
2. false
3. true
4. true
5. false
6. an analogy.
7. eliminates numbers at the extreme end of the range, thus it is more realistic.
8. fact
9. peer
10. she demonstrates that she has first hand experience.

CHAPTER 9: ORGANIZING YOUR IDEAS

Activity 9.1: Using Traditional Patterns

Identify one or more organizational patterns that you could use, given the following specific purposes.

To inform my audience about controversies surrounding campus parking issues.

To entertain my audience with accounts of dating disasters.

To persuade my audience to go on a low carbohydrate diet.

To inform my audience where they can get good meals at reasonable prices.

To persuade (convince) my audience that condoms are an ineffective form of birth control.

To entertain my audience with stories of professors' bloopers.

To inform my audience how to test their investing IQ.

To inform my audience about the various types of veterinarian specialties including pet psychology, dentistry, and surgery.

To persuade my audience to perform volunteer work.

To persuade my audience that grade inflation is a serious issue that needs to be changed.

Activity 9.2: Developing a Topic in Different Ways

Below you'll find a number of subjects followed by the six traditional organizational patterns. Show how you could develop each topic in at least three different ways. Share your responses with your classmates.

Topic: Eating Disorders

Topical pattern –

Chronological pattern --

Spatial pattern --

Causal pattern --

Pro-con pattern --

Problem-solution pattern --

Topic: Rap Music

Topical pattern --

Chronological pattern --

Spatial pattern --

Causal pattern --

Pro-con pattern --

Problem-solution pattern --

Topic: Global Warming

Topical pattern --

Chronological pattern --

Spatial pattern --

Causal pattern --

Pro-con pattern --

Problem-solution pattern --

Topic: Tuition Increases

Topical pattern --

Chronological pattern --

Spatial pattern --

Causal pattern --

Pro-con pattern --

Problem-solution pattern --

Activity 9.3: The Wave Pattern

Watch a video of Martin Luther King, Jr.'s speech, "I Have a Dream."

Dr. King introduces a number of "wave" crests then elaborates on each. Of course, "I have a dream" is the most famous, but the speech contains many other repetitive phrases that King develops with a series of short examples. In the space below, list each wave crest you hear.

How many themes (wave crests) did you identify? ________ Were you surprised by this? Why or why not?

This *could* have been called the "Bank of Justice" speech. How does King develop that metaphor early in the speech? Why do you think his listeners have consistently titled the speech "I Have a Dream" rather than the "Bank of Justice"?

Activity 9.4: Alternative Pattern: The Spiral

The spiral pattern is useful for speeches that build in dramatic intensity. Below each topic, identify at least three spirals that a speaker might use. The first one is done for you.

Topic: Building a New Home

Spiral 1: A simple, standard design three bedroom home is least expensive and easiest to build.

Spiral 2: A larger custom home requires more attention to details and costs more money.

Spiral 3: A very large designer home is most expensive and elaborate, usually requiring consultation with a number of professionals.

Topic: Planning a Vacation

Spiral 1:

Spiral 2:

Spiral 3:

Topic: Weddings

Spiral 1:

Spiral 2:

Spiral 3:

Topic: Working with Children Who've Been Injured in Car Accidents

Spiral 1:

Spiral 2:

Spiral 3:

Topic: Writing a Book

Spiral 1:

Spiral 2:

Spiral 3:

Before You Take the Exam

To test your knowledge and comprehension of organizational principles, review Chapter 9, be able to define key terms, and answer these review questions. Go to http://communication.wadsworth.com/jaffe for an interactive list of key terms.)

1. Give three general tips for organizing main points.

2. Explain the following organizational patterns: topical, chronological, spatial, causal, problem-solution, pro-con.

3. Explain the value of alternative organizational patterns.

4. Describe the wave pattern.

5. Explain the spiral pattern and give examples of ways it can be used effectively.

6. Describe the star organizational pattern.

Test Questions

1. The spatial pattern is the most commonly used organizational pattern. (161)
   - ❍ True
   - ❍ False

2. The problem-solution pattern works well for both informative and persuasive speeches. (161)
   - ❍ True
   - ❍ False

3. Organic organizational patterns are typically used by presidential candidates in formal debates. (163)
   - ❍ True
   - ❍ False

4. The organic pattern most useful for material that builds in dramatic intensity is the wave pattern. (165)
   - ❍ True
   - ❍ False

5. If you were to speak in Madagascar, you'd be expected to begin by making excuses for your inadequacy to speak. (160)
   - ❍ True
   - ❍ False

6. Which is the best reason for limiting your main points? (156)
   - ❍ People learn better when material is chunked into just a few points.
   - ❍ It takes half as much time to prepare a speech with four points instead of eight.
   - ❍ Audiences like shorter speeches.
   - ❍ Good central ideas have only two to four main goals.

7. Which is NOT a tip for organizing your main points? (156-157)
   - ❍ Use evidence to support each main point.
   - ❍ Use a topical pattern whenever you can.
   - ❍ Limit your number of main points to five.
   - ❍ Arrange the order of your points for maximum impact.

8. These points are organized using the _________ pattern: Crack cocaine usage is increasing in the United States; the result is that crime goes up, the users miss out on educational opportunities, and health care costs increase for treatment. (159)
   - ❍ chronological
   - ❍ topical
   - ❍ problem-solution
   - ❍ causal

9. Which central idea does not match the given organizational pattern? (157-161)
   - ❍ Pro-con: Proponents of fetal tissue transplantation have three major arguments; opponents counter with three arguments of their own.
   - ❍ Problem-solution: Many people are sleep deprived; individuals must do something to get more sleep.
   - ❍ Chronological: A good student needs self-discipline, good study habits, and hard work.
   - ❍ Spatial: Exercises can target the upper arms, the legs, and the abdomen.

10. The star pattern is a variation of the ____ pattern. (666)
   - ❍ topical
   - ❍ chronological
   - ❍ pro-con
   - ❍ wave

Answer Bank

1. false
2. true
3. false
4. false
5. true
6. People learn better when material is chunked into just a few points.
7. Use a topical pattern whenever you can.
8. causal
9. Chronological: A good student needs self-discipline, good study habits, and hard work.
10. topical

CHAPTER 10: BEGINNING AND ENDING YOUR SPEECH

Activity 10.1: Gaining Attention

Which item would you most likely use to gain your classmates' attention in an informative speech about volcanoes? (Write "M" in the blank beside the item.) Why? Which would you least likely use? (Write "L" in the blank.) Why?

___ About 550 active volcanoes exist on land--perhaps twice that number under the sea. If they all blew up tomorrow, they would endanger about 10% of the world's population.

___ Since 1983, Kilauea, a volcano in Hawaii, has buried almost 40 square miles and 180 houses; mercifully, no one's been killed.

_ A major volcano is coming, and it will kill by ice, mixed with rocks, mud, dust, and ashes--a mixture harder to escape than 2,000 degree lava.

___ In 1993 Stanley Williams was taking samples from a volcano--a procedure this geologist likens to "walking with a bottle up to the back of a jet as it's taking off." The volcano blew--melting his flashlight, breaking his legs, crushing his skull, and killing nine other people.

Source: Jerry Adler, (1996, May 5). Magma force. Newsweek. *pp. 57-58.*

Which item would you most likely use ("M" in the blank) to gain attention in a classroom persuasive speech about "road rage"? Why? Which would you least likely use ("L" in the blank)? Why?

___ You can't drive if you're blind, or blind drunk. But there are no laws against driving in a blind rage.

___ In June of 1997, the American Automobile Association submitted a report to the American public about the dangers of driving while angry.

___ Aggressive tailgating, headlight flashing, obscene gestures, assaults with weapons ranging from partially eaten burritos or golf clubs to other vehicles. . . you may recognize some of these manifestations of road rage.

___ According to the American Automobile Association, "motorists . . . are increasingly being shot, stabbed, beaten and run over" by other motorists whose rage--road rage--gets out of control.

Source: Jerry Adler. (1997, June 2). "Road rage": We're driven to destruction. Newsweek. *p. 70.*

Which item would you most likely use ("M" in the blank)to gain attention in a classroom persuasive speech about "chocolate"? Why? Which would you least likely use ("L" in the blank)? Why?

___ Good news! New research shows that chocolate contains flavonoids, natural compounds that improve blood flow and keep hearts healthy.

___ When is a kiss more than a kiss? When it's made of chocolate! New research shows that chocolate may actually be good for you.

___ [Pile up 12.2 pounds of chocolate bars and other candies, then say] On the average, Americans consume 12.2 pounds of chocolate every year.

___ Chocolate-loving European immigrants settled in Pennsylvania in the 19th century; the state has always been the nation's chocolate capital, producing almost one sixth of the chocolate we eat annually.

Source: Kim Clark. (2000, April 24). Chocolate pilgrims find paradise in Pennsylvania. U.S. News, *p. 72.*

Activity 10.2: Relating to the Audience

How would you relate the following topics to your classmates?

- the benefits of eating a low fat diet
- the comparatively large amount of pollution caused by sport utility vehicles
- the use of a medical, nontoxic form of super glue to close wounds in emergency room patients
- the legacy of Elvis Presley
- high school clubs for gay, lesbian, bi-sexual, and transgendered students
- upcoming blockbuster summer movies
- the effectiveness or ineffectiveness of the current Vice-President of the United States
- the value of reading aloud to young children
- tips for safe investing in the stock market
- the cultural impact of online pornography

Get together with a small group within your class, and share your responses. Decide which ways to relate to the audience would probably be most effective in your classroom.

Activity 10.3: Establishing Your Credibility on a Topic

How would you establish your credibility on the following topics?

- the benefits of exercise
- how to manage stress
- the cost of tuition
- the legacy of Elvis Presley
- the controversy over the Pledge of Allegiance
- the Israel-Palestine issue
- the effectiveness or ineffectiveness of the current President of the United States
- the value of reading aloud to young children
- the cultural impact of online shopping

Get together with a small group within your class, and share your responses. Decide which ways to relate to the audience would probably be most effective in your classroom.

Activity 10.4: Connecting the Parts of the Speech

Below you'll find an outline of a student speech. Work with another member of the class to write connectives between the parts of the speech.

Introduction

I. On November 10, 1984, I arrived in the U. S. to meet my adoptive family.
II. Someday you may be in the position of adopting a child.
III. I was adopted when I was a teenager, living in an orphanage in the Philippines.
IV. Today, I will discuss the steps for adopting a child from another country: application, selection of child, child arrival, and postplacement.

Body

I. [Signpost] ________________________________ application step.
 A. The agency sends information.
 B. You fill in an application.
 C. You work with the agency to evaluate your suitability to adopt.

II. [Signpost] ________________________________ selection step.
 A. Your name goes on a waiting list.
 B. A social worker sends you pictures and information about a child.
 C. You select a child and sign a Placement Agreement Form.

[Transition]____

____

III. Child Arrival.
 A. Apply for an "Orphan Visa" to bring your child into the U. S.
 B. An escort brings the child (and other children) to the U. S.
 C. The family gets medical insurance for the child.

Internal Summary: ____

____

IV. Postplacement.
 A. For 6 months to a year, the social worker works with your family.
 B. The child is legally adopted.

Conclusion

I. In conclusion, application, selection, child arrival, and postplacement are the steps you go through in adopting a child from overseas.
II. Although this may seem like a lot of work, I am grateful that my parents did it.
III. Without them, I would probably still be in an orphanage in the Philippines.

Marieta Cribbins. The adoption process. Oregon State University.

Before You Take the Exam

To test your knowledge and comprehension of introductions and conclusions, review Chapter 10, be able to define key terms, and answer these review questions. Go to site http://communication.wadsworth.com/jaffe for an interactive list of key terms.

1. List and explain four elements of effective introductions.
2. Name and give examples of eight ways to draw attention to a subject.
3. Give examples of ways that speakers adapt their introductory strategies to accommodate diversity in organizations or in cultural groups.
4. List and explain four elements to include in effective conclusions.
5. Describe the value of an "echo" or repetition of material presented more than once in a speech.
6. List a number of ways to end a speech memorably.
7. Be able to explain the characteristics of signposts, transitions, internal previews, and internal summaries.

Sample Test Questions

1. A quotation used to draw attention to a topic should be from a well-known source. (178)
   - ❍ True
   - ❍ False
2. Jokes rarely fail, because most people listen intently when humor is involved. (179)
   - ❍ True
   - ❍ False
3. Navajo students usually show visual aids to begin their speeches. (183)
   - ❍ True
   - ❍ False
4. An echo or loop back to something in the introduction of the speech provides psychological closure for your ideas. (185)
   - ❍ True
   - ❍ False
5. "Most importantly . . . " is an example of a signpost. (188)
   - ❍ True
   - ❍ False

6. Which is NOT explained in the text as a way to draw attention to a subject at the beginning of a speech? (176)
   - ❍ Ask a rhetorical question.
   - ❍ Give a quotation from your high school basketball coach.
   - ❍ Show a dramatic photograph that illustrates the subject.
   - ❍ Say, "Today my talk will be about . . . "

7. Which of the following is a way to relate the topic to the audience? (181-182)
   - ❍ The French artist Monet said, "I think as the bird sings."
   - ❍ As an admirer of Monet and an art major, I have learned some interesting facts about his painting techniques.
   - ❍ Whether or not you know his name, you have probably seen his art.
   - ❍ Today, I'll explain three defining aspects of Monet's body of work.

8. Which is NOT given in the text as a way to end a speech memorably? (186)
   - ❍ Review the main ideas.
   - ❍ Issue a challenge.
   - ❍ Tie the subject to a larger cultural theme or value.
   - ❍ Ask a thought-provoking question.

9. Which of the following is a transition statement? (188)
   - ❍ The final element of Monet's technique is his broad, fragmented brush strokes.
   - ❍ Now that you're aware of his focus on nature, let's look at his palette of hues.
   - ❍ First, Monet focused on nature.
   - ❍ Monet's use of color was unique in two ways: his colors were unmixed and his hues were vibrant.

10. Which element of an introduction is sometimes optional? (183)
    - ❍ Gain attention.
    - ❍ Relate to the audience.
    - ❍ Establish your credibility to speak on the topic.
    - ❍ Preview your main ideas.

Answer Bank

1. false
2. false
3. false
4. true
5. true
6. Say, "Today my talk will be about . . . "
7. Whether or not you know his name, you have probably seen his art.
8. Review the main ideas.
9. Now that you're aware of his focus on nature, let's look at his palette of hues.
10. Establish your credibility to speak on the topic.

CHAPTER 11: PUTTING IT ALL TOGETHER: OUTLINING YOUR SPEECH

Activity 11.1: Study a Sample Format -- Content Outline

Students across the country commonly use a linear outline format such as the following. Use this format to guide you as you create your own content outlines.

Headings
Title:
General Purpose:
Specific Purpose:
Central Idea:

Introduction

I. Gain attention.

II. Relate to the audience.

III. Establish your credibility.

IV. Preview your main points.

Body

I. Main point
  A. Supporting material
    1. Specific information (such as a statistic)
    2. Specific information (such as a quotation)
  B. Supporting material

II. Main point
  A. Supporting material
  B. Supporting material
    1. Specific information (such as a statistic)
    2. Specific information (such as a quotation)
      a.) Very specific information for this subpoint
      b.) Additional very specific information

Conclusion

I. Signal the end.

II. Review your main points.

III. Tie to the introduction.

IV. End with impact.

References
Include three or more sources, depending on the assignment. You'll find the APA or MLA bibliographic source citation guidelines online or in the reference section of your library.

Activity 11.2: Sample Outline--Biographical Speech

As you read through this content outline, you'll find specific questions after major sections. Evaluate the outline by using principles found in Chapter 11 and in Activity 11.1.

Topic:	Hector Berlioz
General Purpose:	To inform
Specific Purpose:	To inform my audience about the Romantic composer, Hector Berlioz.
Central Idea:	Hector Berlioz was a true romantic composer who introduced important ideas into music composition.

Does this heading include all the important information described in your text?

Introduction

I. [Play a 15-second clip of Berlioz's music during points I & II of the introduction.] (Voice over, pausing between words) unearthly sounds . . . nighttime . . . distant horn calls . . . summoning . . .

II. Most of us have experienced this haunting effect.

   A. Possibly we've read or heard a horror story--or we've heard this type of background music during a scary movie.

   B. Hector Berlioz was the musician who created such effects in music.

III. As a musician trained in piano, clarinet, and guitar, I attended Fiorello H. LaGuardia of Music and Art High School where I was required to study music history and research the lives of musicians and composers.

IV. I will share with you some aspects of Hector Berlioz's fascinating biography and explain the important contributions he made in music composition.

Is enough detail included that you know the general direction of the speech? Is too much detail presented?

Body

I. To understand him, we must go back in time to the early 19th century commonly remembered as the Romantic Period.

[Display drawing of Berlioz that has been transferred to a transparency.]

   A. Berlioz was born in 1803 into a well-to-do physician's family, during a period when romantic poets and writers dominated literature.

      1. As a child he read travel books and longed for adventures in faraway countries.

      2. He learned flute and guitar, but never the piano.

      3. He learned harmony from books without reference to a keyboard.

4. When he was 12, like a true romantic, he fell passionately in love with an 18-year-old who influenced his first compositions--at age 13.

B. When he was ready for university studies, his father sent him to Paris to study to be a doctor like himself.

1. Instead Hector could not imagine dissecting rats--and human bodies.

2. He decided to abandon medicine (and parental funds) and attend the Paris Conservatory of Music.

C. One night at the theater, he fell madly in love from afar with an actress named Harriet Smithson--and with Shakespearean plays.

1. According to rumor, he followed her theater group performances.

2. Eventually they married, but the reality of marriage did not match his romantic notions of it.

3. His passion for Shakespeare inspired major works on *Hamlet* and *The Tempest.*

II. His temperament led to musical innovations.

A. One is the *idée fixe*, or dominant theme, that recurs throughout a Berlioz symphony.

1. The idea of a dominant, recurring theme ties into Romanticism.

2. It is linked to his obsessive love for Harriet; he made her his *idée fixe* in one of his greatest symphonies, *the Fantastic Symphony.*

3. The composer varies the theme by adjusting pace, pitch, meter, or orchestration.

4. This is the dominant theme that recurs throughout that symphony.

<u>[Play short excerpt --then cut to a variation that appears later.]</u>

B. Another innovation was the five movement "grandiose" symphony, instead of the usual four movement piece.

C. Berlioz also used instruments in imaginative ways; for example plucking violins created the sound of flying bats.

<u>[Play an excerpt that demonstrates this.]</u>

D. He was keenly aware of the importance of matching sound to space.

1. He disliked large orchestras in small spaces.

2. But in large spaces, he used 120-piece orchestras to create a massive sound, uncommon in his time.

<u>[Play a short musical clip that illustrates this.]</u>

Does the outline fulfill the goals set forth in the heading? If so, how? If not, why not?

Conclusion

I. In conclusion, this true Romantic broke new ground with his original ideas, and he has inspired many composers.

II. In his time, his massive orchestra was too awkward, the five movements made his symphonies long and boring, and his odd use of instruments for sound effects was unappreciated.

III. However, he is appreciated today precisely for his eccentric innovations.

IV. And what is a horror movie without the music that evokes our fears?

Does the conclusion include all the necessary elements? Is new information added? What changes, if any, would you make to any part of this outline?

References

Berlioz, H. (1865). *The memoirs of Hector Berlioz: Member of the French Institute including his travels in Italy, Germany, Russia, and England.* (D. Cairn, Trans, Ed.) New York: W. W. Norton.

Berlioz, H. (1956). *Symphonie Fantastique, Op. 14* [sound recording]. Berliner Philharmoniker. Herbert von Karajan (conductor). Deutsche Grammophon.

Holoman, D. K. (1989). *Berlioz.* Cambridge: Harvard University Press.

Kerman, J. (1987). *Listen: Brief edition.* New York: Worth Publishers.

Sadie, S. (Ed.) (1980). *The new Grove dictionary of music and musicians (Vol. 2).* Washington, DC: Grove.

Tepper, M. B. (1995, November 29, last updated). Foreward to the 1995 HTML edition: Tempo, style, and options in modern performances of Hector Berlioz' *Grande Messe des morts, Op. 5.* Master's Thesis. University of Minnesota, 1983. Available online: http://home.earthlink.net/~oy/foreword.htm

Yesenia Abreu, St. John's University

What bibliographic formatting style is Yesenia using? Is her information correctly cited? (To check this, go online to www.google.com *and look up the exact phrase* APA Style Manual *and* MLA Style Manual.*)*

Activity 11.3: Creating Speaking Notes

On the four note cards below, create a set of speaking notes for the speech about Hector Berlioz featured in Activity 11.2.

Introduction

Body: Main Point I

Body: Main Point II

Conclusion

Activity 11.4: Unscramble an Outline

Unscramble the outline below. Then discuss with your classmates the cues you used to decide what material went into the introduction, the main points, the supporting materials, and the conclusion. (This outline was prepared by Nila Sheth at St. John's University, Queens)

Specific Purpose: To inform my audience how to gather, report, and assess information on the 1040 tax form.

Group your expenses into appropriate categories.

Would your 1040 hold up during an audit?

The first step, collecting and classifying your tax data, is probably the most difficult.

The most important piece of information is the W-2 Wage Statement that your employer mails in January.

You also need a 1040 form which you'll find in the tax packet that the IRS mails out.

Information reported on the 1040 form must have back-up support, in case of future audit.

Report all income in the income section—even trivial amounts.

Many people dread it as the deadline for filing tax returns; however, everyone who receives a W-2 wage must file, and most people want to save money on the process.

Don't skip any lines' this may cause miscalculation.

Today, I will show you how to fill out the 1040 form by collecting data, disclosing information, and assessing the aftereffects of the process.

False information may lead to a fine, even imprisonment.

The second step is to disclose all relevant information on the 1040 form.

Fill in the sections reporting any accumulated interest.

I am majoring in finance, and I learned through my courses and my experiences that filing a return is not as hard as others make it seem.

Be sure to sign your return; it is void with no signature.

Finally, determine the aftereffects of turning in a false or dishonest return.

Collect receipts of additional income and taxable expenses.

If you expect a refund, it may take up to twelve weeks to get a check in the mail.

In short, the 1040 is a standard form each American worker must file.

Were you completely truthful?

It is simple enough that you can fill it out yourself by collecting and classifying important material, filling in every applicable section, and taking seriously the consequences of false returns.

April 15—what does that date mean to you?

April 15—don't forget this date—it will never change; it's a date the IRS looks forward to!

Activity 11.5: Use the Spiral Pattern

Return to Activity 9.3 and select one of the topics you developed in a spiral pattern. On the diagram below, show how you might create a spiral outline for the subject you select.

Activity 11.6: Use a Star Pattern

Plan out a four-part speech with a topical organization, and try your hand at using a star outline. (See Figure 9.5 in the text.) Be sure to write out the theme of the speech around the points of the star.

Ideas:
Caring for a pet (four things necessary to maintaining a healthy, happy animal)
Qualities of a friend (select four qualities you consider essential, define each one, and give examples of each)
Required courses in your major (select four courses, describe course content, and tell why the material is vital to the occupation you plan to enter)

Before You Take the Exam

To test your knowledge and comprehension of principles of outlining, review Chapter 11, be able to define key terms, and answer these review questions. (Follow links to the Jaffe text on the Communication Café web site http://communication.wadsworth.com for an interactive list of key terms.)

1. Distinguish between a rough draft outline, a script, a content outline, and speaking notes.
2. Describe the elements of a heading.
3. Explain the principles of coordination, indentation, parallel points, and subordination.
4. Be able to cite sources correctly, using the format your instructor requires.
5. Be able to create a key word outline, given a content outline.
6. Provide tips for creating note cards.
7. Provide tips for creating a speaking outline.
8. Identify elements of cognitive style that affects the way people create outlines.

Sample Questions

1. A content outline is the same as a speaking outline. (196)
   ❍ True
   ❍ False

2. The principle of coordination means that your supporting points are placed under your major points. (197)
   ❍ True
   ❍ False

3. Using color on your speaking notes or outlines can help you keep your place in your speech. (203)
   ❍ True
   ❍ False

4. Left-brain thinking processes are more linear. (208)
   ❍ True
   ❍ False

5. When using a star or spiral outlining format, you should still use standard indentation and numbering so that you always know how your speech elements relate to one another. (205)
   ❍ True
   ❍ False

6. Which is NOT a part of the heading for your outline? (206)
   - ❍ the general purpose
   - ❍ parallel points
   - ❍ the specific purpose statement
   - ❍ A title
   - ❍ the central idea

7. Which is NOT a principle of outlining? (207)
   - ❍ Alternate numbers and letters within the outline.
   - ❍ Coordinate your points.
   - ❍ Use phrases for main points and sentences for supporting material.
   - ❍ Subordinate first-level points under major points.

8. In your content outline, __________ (196-199)
   - ❍ separate your transitions from your lettering and numbering system.
   - ❍ indent only your major points.
   - ❍ use the following pattern for your points: I. . . . 1. . . . (1) . . . i. . . . .
   - ❍ use color to highlight major points.

9. In contrast to content outlines, speaking outlines should contain __________ (202-204)
   - ❍ only the main points in the body of the speech.
   - ❍ helpful delivery hints scattered throughout.
   - ❍ complete declarative sentences.
   - ❍ indentation that helps you see the coordination and subordination of your materials.

10. Another term for thinking style is ________ (208)
    - ❍ cognitive style.
    - ❍ individual style.
    - ❍ personal style.
    - ❍ cultural style.

Answer Bank

1. false
2. false
3. true
4. true
5. false
6. parallel points
7. Use phrases for main points and sentences for supporting material.
8. separate your transitions from your lettering and numbering system.
9. helpful delivery hints scattered throughout.
10. cognitive style.

CHAPTER 12: VISUAL AIDS: FROM CHALKBOARD TO COMPUTER

Activity 12.1: Check List for Visual or Audio Aids (VAs)

Before you speak, check the ones that apply from the list below.

___ Is this VA necessary?

___ Is it the best VA for the content of the speech?

___ Is it clear?

___ Have I crossed out any unnecessary words on my visual?

___ Is the visual professional looking, no "loving hands at home" look?

___ Have I paid attention to size and spacing of information on the visual?

___ Is the visual uncluttered?

___ Have I used color to advantage?

___ Will the visual be visible to everyone in the room?

___ Will the visual be displayed only when it's discussed? (e.g. Do I have blank slides between the word slides?)

___ Is the audio or videotape cued up precisely?

___ Will the necessary presentation equipment be in the classroom? If not, do I know how to order it?

___ Do I know how to use the equipment?

___ Have I practiced using this VA?

___ Does the VA supplement, not replace, my words?

___ Do I have a Plan B in case something goes wrong?

Activity 12.2: Evaluating Computer-Created Visuals

Tell how to make each visual more effective.

Stages of Grief
Denial
Anger
Bargaining
Depression
Acceptance

Stages of Grief

- **Denial**
- **Anger**
- **Bargaining**
- **Depression**
- **Acceptance**

Stages of Grief

- Denial
- **Anger**
- Bargaining
- **Depression**
- **Acceptance**

Stages of Grief

In the first stage, denial, the person refuses to accept that someone is dying.

Next, the person typically gets angry--at the doctors, at the person, at God.

The third stage involves bargaining that goes something like this: "If he just gets well, I'll be the best daughter in the whole world."

When the realization sets in that death is unavoidable, the person becomes depressed.

Finally, the grieving person accepts the loss.

Activity 12.3: Evaluate a Presentation that Uses VAs

According to a January 22, 2003 article from the Knight Ridder News Service, a Microsoft spokesperson estimated that more than 30,000,000 PowerPoint presentations take place daily around the world! The program was developed for use in businesses, but since 1998, educators have been incorporating more and more PowerPoint presentations into their lectures.

Add to that the thousands of overhead transparencies, the number of videotape clips, the numerous handouts and the millions of boards in use in organizations and institutions and you realize the widespread use of visuals to support presentations.

Attend two lectures or speeches that incorporate visual aids and compare and contrast the ways the presenter used the visuals.

	Presenter 1	**Presenter 2**
Type(s) of visuals used?		
Neatness of the visual?		
Use of color?		
Follows guidelines?		
Displayed well?		
Overall effectiveness?		
Suggestions for improvement?		

Activity 12.4: Adapting Visuals to Audiences and Situations

Work with a small group of your classmates. Given the following speech occasions, come up with a visual aid plan that fits the audience and the situation described in each scenario.

Because of the speechmaking abilities you've developed through this course, you have been asked to give a presentation about how to use the campus library and Internet sources to do research. (You'll be covering the basic concepts found in Chapter 7 of the text).

Audience #1: Foreign students who are taking their first speech class after going through an ESL program at your university.

- Select from this list all the audio or visual support you would use: __ objects, __ persons, __ models, __ lists, __ tables, __ charts, __ graphs, __ photographs, __ drawings, __ maps, __ videos, or __ audiotapes.

- How effective would a tour be with this group?

- Specifically describe your visual package. (What parts of your presentation would you support with visuals or audiotapes? What, specifically, would you put on the visuals? What videotapes or audiotapes would you use? If you chose to go on a tour, where would you stop and explain library or Internet research?)

Audience #2: alumni visiting your school twenty or thirty years after they graduated.

- Select from this list all the audio or visual support you would use: __ objects, __ persons, __ models, __ lists, __ tables, __ charts, __ graphs, __ photographs, __ drawings, __ maps, __ videos, or __ audiotapes.

- How effective would a tour be with this group?

- Specifically describe your visual package. (What parts of your presentation would you support with visuals or audiotapes? What, specifically, would you put on the visuals? What videotapes or audiotapes would you use? If you chose to go on a tour, where would you stop and explain library or Internet research?)

Audience #3: a "talented and gifted" class of eighth graders who have come to your campus to take advantages of the resources your library has to offer them.

- Select from this list all the audio or visual support you would use: __ objects, __ persons, __ models, __ lists, __ tables, __ charts, __ graphs, __ photographs, __ drawings, __ maps, __ videos, or __ audiotapes.

- How effective would a tour be with this group?

- Specifically describe your visual package. (What parts of your presentation would you support with visuals or audiotapes? What, specifically, would you put on the visuals? What videotapes or audiotapes would you use? If you chose to go on a tour, where would you stop and explain library or Internet research?)

Activity 12.5: Evaluating the Use of Visual Aids

Use visuals available from Wadsworth to watch the following speeches and evaluate the speaker's use of visual aids in each.

Watch the speech "Impressionistic Painting" (Student Speeches Video, Volume I). Because the original speaker was unavailable to tape the speech, the speaker you see, Chris Lucke, adapted and presented this speech written by Wendy Finkelmen of the University of Cincinnati. After your viewing, answer the following questions:

- In your opinion, are visual aids essential or optional, given this topic? Why?
- Do you think Chris's (and Wendy's) choice of visual support was adequate? What might you omit? What might you add?
- Was the visual material explained clearly? If not, what could be done differently?
- How effective was the visual support? What might the speaker do to make the visuals even more effective?

Watch Shaura Neil's speech on the CD-ROM that comes packaged with your text. (The script of the speech is included at the end of Chapter 12). Then answer the following questions:

- In your opinion, are visual aids essential or optional, given this topic? Why?
- Do you think Shaura's choice of visual support is adequate? What might you omit? What might you add?
- Did she explain her visual material clearly? If not, what could she do differently?
- How effective was the visual support? What might she do to make the visuals even more effective?

If these speeches are unavailable, watch two visual aid speeches of your choice and answer the above questions regarding them.

Before You Take the Exam

To test your knowledge and comprehension of visual aids, review Chapter 12, be able to define key terms, and answer the following review questions. Go to http://communication.wadsworth.com/jaffe for an interactive list of key terms.

1. Explain why visual aids are useful in all cultures.
2. List advantages of visual aids to nonnative speakers of English and their audiences.
3. Know the advantages and disadvantages of the following types of presentation technology: overhead projectors, chalk and whiteboards, handouts, poster boards and flip charts, slides projectors, computer projection systems.
4. Give tips for using the following types of presentation technology: overhead projectors, chalk and whiteboards, handouts, poster boards and flip charts, slides projectors, computer projection systems.
5. Describe some issues that speakers face when they take their visual aids to other countries.
6. Identify ways that the following types of visuals are useful: objects, models, people, lists, charts, flowchart, organizational charts, line graphs, bar graphs, pie graphs, pictographs, photographs, drawings, political maps, and geographic maps.
7. Provide tips for using the following types of visuals: objects, models, people, lists, charts, flowchart, organizational charts, line graphs, bar graphs, pie graphs, pictographs, photographs, drawings, political maps, and geographic maps.
8. Distinguish between text-based visuals and image-based visuals.
9. Identify speech occasions in which audio support is helpful.
10. Give tips for using video resources successfully.
11. Describe the following: graphics programs, presentation programs, scanners.
12. Provide design tips for visual aids, considering fonts, readability, size and spacing, and use of color and emphasis.
13. Give seven general tips for using audio and visual aids effectively.

Sample Test Questions

1. The way you use your visuals can add to your audience's perception of your credibility. (229)
   - ❍ True
   - ❍ False
2. Handouts make a good Plan B to use in case of equipment failure. (229)
   - ❍ True
   - ❍ False

3. Using color on your visuals tends to distract the audience from your main points. (228)
   - ❍ True
   - ❍ False

4. Pie graphs are image-based visuals. (221)
   - ❍ True
   - ❍ False

5. Using video or audio support is too complicated for most classroom speeches. (224)
   - ❍ True
   - ❍ False

6. The best visual for an insurance salesperson to use when she is in a couple's home, trying to convince them to buy a policy is probably a(n) __________ featuring graphs, drawings, and informational lists. (214)
   - ❍ table sized flip chart
   - ❍ series of overhead transparencies
   - ❍ set of slides
   - ❍ audiotape

7. All of these classroom topics would probably go well with objects as support, EXCEPT ___ (219)
   - ❍ how to improve your golf swing.
   - ❍ brewing the perfect cup of tea.
   - ❍ how to put a trigger lock on a gun.
   - ❍ how to do a magic trick.

8. A ____ graph would be best for a speech showing the direction of the stock market during the decade of the 1990s. (221)
   - ❍ line
   - ❍ bar
   - ❍ pie
   - ❍ picture

9. Photographs are useful visual aids only if they are _________ (221)
   - ❍ close-up shots of the subject.
   - ❍ large enough for your audience to see their details.
   - ❍ in color.
   - ❍ distributed on a handout to each member of the audience.

10. A major principle for well-designed visual aids is: (228)
    - ❍ Simplify, simplify, simplify.
    - ❍ Prepare at least five coordinated visuals for your talk.
    - ❍ Vary the font from visual to visual.
    - ❍ Use green as an emphasis color.
    - ❍ Use a transition for every slide in order to keep the audience's attention.

Answer Bank

1. true
2. true
3. false
4. true
5. false
6. table sized flip chart
7. how to put a trigger lock on a gun.
8. line
9. large enough for your audience to see their details.
10. Simplify, simplify, simplify.

CHAPTER 13: CHOOSING EFFECTIVE LANGUAGE

Activity 13.1 Vivid Language

President John Kennedy's Inaugural Address is widely acclaimed as a model of excellent language. (His major speechwriter, Theodore Sorensen, is responsible for many of the vivid images.) Read the beginning and ending of the speech, and underline memorable or vivid phrases. Be prepared to discuss with your classmates the stylistic devices he uses (e.g. alliteration, repetition, metaphors, and so on).

Vice President Johnson, Mr. Speaker, Mr. Chief Justice, President Eisenhower, Vice President Nixon, President Truman, Reverend Clergy, fellow citizens:

We observe today not a victory of party but a celebration of freedom--symbolizing an end as well as a beginning--signifying renewal as well as change. For I have sworn before you and Almighty God the same solemn oath our forbears prescribed nearly a century and three-quarters ago.

The world is very different now. For man holds in his mortal hands the power to abolish all forms of human poverty and all forms of human life. And yet the same revolutionary beliefs for which our forebears fought are still at issue around the globe--the belief that the rights of man come not from the generosity of the state but from the hand of God.

We dare not forget today that we are the heirs of that first revolution. Let the word go forth from this time and place, to friend and foe alike, that the torch has been passed to a new generation of Americans--born in this century, tempered by war, disciplined by a hard and bitter peace, proud of our ancient heritage--and unwilling to witness or permit the slow undoing of those human rights to which this nation has always been committed, and to which we are committed today at home and around the world.

Let every nation know, whether it wishes us well or ill, that we shall pay any price, bear any burden, meet any hardship, support any friend, oppose any foe to assure the survival and the success of liberty.

This much we pledge--and more. . . .

In the long history of the world, only a few generations have been granted the role of defending freedom in its hour of maximum danger. I do not shrink from this responsibility--I welcome it. I do not believe that any of us would exchange places with any other people or any other generation. The energy, the faith, the devotion which we bring to this endeavor will light our country and all who serve it--and the glow from that fire can truly light the world.

And so, my fellow Americans: ask not what your country can do for you--ask what you can do for your country.

My fellow citizens of the world: ask not what America will do for you, but what together we can do for the freedom of man.

Finally, whether you are citizens of America or citizens of the world, ask of us here the same high standards of strength and sacrifice which we ask of you. With a good conscience our only sure reward, with history the final judge of our deeds, let us go forth to lead the land we love, asking His blessing and His help, but knowing that here on earth God's work must truly be our own.

(You can hear or read this entire speech online; google.com will help you locate it.)

Activity 13.2: Use of Imagery

Page 246 in the text states the importance of vivid language that helps listeners see, feel, and remember your speech. Imagery is language that helps listeners imagine or create mental images. You can use five basic types of images that appeal to the senses o: sight, hearing, smell, taste, touch.

The following examples come from student speeches. Underline the vivid images in each, then on the lines below each, write the same sentence(s) in an ordinary (and arguably boring) way.

Have you ever bitten into a fat, juicy, bacon double cheeseburger with onions, pickles, ketchup, mayonnaise, and juices just oozing out? At one time or another, most have probably eaten what I call a heart attack on a bun. (Andrés Lucero)

____

____

Peaceful and serene, quiet and cool, it's a day for fishing with your family. The sun is shining on your face, the wind blowing softly on your body, and there are no worries of work, traffic, or the bustle of city life. (Jill Nagaue)

____

____

I watched everyone being sucked out of the plane as I scooted toward the plexiglass sliding door. The moment had arrived! Within an instant, I was free-falling at 100 mph. Forty-five seconds later the parachute jerked a little and we slowed to about seven mph. (Allison Sherbo)

____

____

Imagine you're shopping in a grocery store. In the candy aisle, you notice a child pulling on her mother's sleeve. "Mommy, I want candy. CANDY! CANDY! CANDY!" The mother responds, "OK, honey, but stop screaming!" In frozen foods, you hear a second child howling. His mother grabs him by the arm, whacks him on the behind, and yells, BE QUIET!" (Anna McInturf)

____

____

Gerard [Majella] had a weak, delicate appearance and seemed more of a ghost than a man. He was long and lanky and had an emaciated face. (Daniel Kelly)

____

Activity 13.3: Eliminate Clutter

This speech draft contains many unnecessary words. Working with a partner, eliminate the clutter. In some cases, you may have to reword the sentence slightly.

WHEN ONE MENTIONS THE WORD DESTINY, IT AUTOMATICALLY CONJURES UP A VISION OF SOMETHING BEYOND THE POWER/CONTROL OF ORDINARY HUMANS. INDIVIDUALS HAVE OFTEN REFERRED TO DESTINY AS AN UNAVOIDABLE LOT, FATE, OR EVEN DOOM THAT HAS ALREADY BEEN PREDETERMINED BY SOME IRRESISTIBLE POWER.

THE ROMANS USED TO HAVE A LATIN SAYING: '*DESTINATUM EST MINI*," MEANING, "I HAVE MADE UP MY MIND." HERE, DESTINY STOOD FOR AN ACT THAT WAS FIXED OR DETERMINED. LATER ON, WE SEE THE WORD REAPPEARING IN BOTH THE OLD AND MIDDLE FRENCH VOCABULARY IN THE FEMININE FORM "*DESTINE*." FINALLY, FROM THE MIDDLE ENGLISH WORD "*DESTINEE*" WHICH WAS SPELLED WITH A DOUBLE "E" AT THE END"), WE GET THE MODERN DAY FORM OF THE WORD AS WE KNOW IT TODAY.

HOWEVER, IT ISN'T A WORD'S ETYMOLOGICAL HISTORY WE SEE WHEN WE READ OR USE A SPECIFIC WORD. MANY TIMES WE DON'T SEE OR FEEL ANYTHING AT ALL, BUT, IN CERTAIN INSTANCES, WORDS TEND TO CARRY A DEEPER MEANING. EVEN IF IT IS JUST ONE SINGLE WORD, AS IS THE CASE WITH DESTINY.

Before You Take the Exam

To test your knowledge and comprehension of language issues, review Chapter 13, be able to define key terms, and answer the following review questions. Go to http://communication.wadsworth.com/Jaffe for an interactive list of key terms.

1. Explain how words are linked to culture and meaning.
2. Tell the difference between denotative and connotative meanings, and give examples of each.
3. Define dialects and jargon; tell when each is appropriate in public speaking.
4. Explain how power is linked to the ability to name or label groups and issues.
5. Define epithets and euphemisms and give examples of each.
6. Describe ageist and sexist language usage.
7. Give six guidelines for language used in public speaking.
8. Explain and give examples of alliteration, rhyme, repetition, personification, hyperbole, metaphor, and simile.
9. Tell the difference between monolingual, bidialectical, multidialectical, bilingual, ant multilingual speakers.
10. Give tips for speaking to a linguistically diverse audience.
11. Tell five ways to be a better listener to a nonnative speaker of English.

Sample Questions

1. More than 10,000 words have been added to the English language since 1961. (238)
   - o True
   - o False
2. "Being downsized" is an epithet for "being fired." (239)
   - o True
   - o False
3. To speak more directly, eliminate verbiage whenever you can. (243)
   - o True
   - o False
4. Rhymes should be used only at the end of sentences. (246-247)
   - o True
   - o False
5. If you speak both French and English, you are bi-dialectical. (266)
   - o True
   - o False

6. On one show, Oprah Winfrey featured "age-defying beauty" in which women, who looked much younger than they actually were, told their beauty secrets. The text would say that Oprah was illustrating the concept of _____ . (241)
   - ageism.
   - hyperbole.
   - connotative language.
   - nonparallel language.

7. According to the text, calling someone a "nerd" is an example of ______ (239)
   - Gen X jargon.
   - an epithet.
   - denotative language.
   - a metaphor.

8. "We want wealth, wisdom, and work from our board members" is an example of ____. (246)
   - rhyming.
   - vague language.
   - alliteration.
   - a mixed metaphor.

9. Which is NOT a key to listening to a non-native speaker of English? (250)
   - Be positive about the speech.
   - Take steps to focus your attention on the speech.
   - Laugh when the speaker laughs at her or his mistakes.
   - Give nonverbal feedback.

10. When adapting to an interpreter, remember to _____. (250)
    - look at the audience throughout the speech, so that your listeners will always be mindful that you are the speaker.
    - give your interpreter your speech outline when you get to the podium.
    - shorten your speech to accommodate the extra time it will take to deliver the speech.
    - present one major idea with its supporting material, then allow the interpreter to speak.

Answer Bank

1. true
2. false
3. true
4. false
5. false
6. ageism.
7. an epithet.
8. alliteration.
9. Laugh when the speaker laughs at her or his mistakes.
10. shorten your speech to accommodate the extra time it will take to deliver the speech.

CHAPTER 14: DELIVERING YOUR SPEECH

Activity 14.1: Evaluating Videotaped Delivery

Watch a videotape of a student speech with the sound turned off. You are forming an impression of the speaker, not through the words of the speech, but through her or his nonverbal communication. Jot down notes in response to these questions as you watch:

Does the speaker have a *physical feature* that causes you to respond in a stereotyped manner? If so, what is it? What's your response?

Evaluate the speaker's *grooming*? In what ways does it enhance or detract from your impression of the speaker?

Assess the appropriateness of the speaker's *clothing* and *accessories* for the audience and the situation.

In what ways are the speaker's *gestures* effective? ineffective?

What *emblems* (if any) do you notice?

What *illustrators* do you observe?

Any *adaptors*?

Evaluate the speaker's *eye contact.*

How effectively does this speaker adapt for the camera?

What, if any, suggestions would you give this speaker to help him or her create a more favorable impression through nonverbal channels?

Activity 14.2: Vocal Variation

Watch a videotape of a public figure who regularly gives speeches. Then answer the following questions. (If you have CNN Today: Public Speaking Election 2000 has a variety of speakers.*) If you watch the CNN tape, watch four speakers, but focus on one specific speaker.*

In what ways, if any, is the ethnicity of the speaker evidenced through his or her pronunciation or enunciation?

Answer the following questions about the speaker's vocal variation:

Which category best describes his or her volume and rate?

___ Loud and fast
___ Loud and slow
___ Soft and fast
___ Soft and slow

What is the overall impression you get of the speaker's personality traits and credibility through these vocal characteristics? (Use pages 263-267 in the text to guide your evaluation.)

Give specific examples of the speaker's effective use of pitch variation or inflection.

Point out specific words or syllables that the speaker stresses effectively.

Evaluate the use of pauses for emphasis or dramatic effect.

Overall, what style does the speaker most embody?

- Confident style -- identify specific things the speaker does that illustrates this style:

- Conversational style -- identify specific ways the speaker demonstrates this style:

Which type of delivery does the speaker use? ___ memorized, ___ impromptu
___ manuscript, ___ extemporaneous

- Why do you think the speaker chose the delivery mode s/he did?

- What would the effect of the speech be if s/he chose another style? For example, how would a memorized speech change if the speaker were reading from a manuscript? Would another style be more appropriate, given the situation?

Activity 14.3: Vary Your Vocalics

Work with three or four others to do this activity. Below are several newspaper want ads (with identifying names and addresses changed). Designate one person as the "voice chooser" (VC); the rest are readers. Have someone begin reading an ad, using a normal voice. The VC breaks into the reading at any point and says "next" (and the person on the left begins reading where the first person left off). The VC also selects a "voice" that the reader will assume. (You'll find several voices at the bottom of the page.)

For example, the VC might say, "next--small child" or "next--sportscaster." Whoever is reading then takes on the vocal characteristics of the child or of the sportscaster. The VC can also ask a single reader to switch voices mid-reading. (Change the Voice Chooser role periodically.)

\- -

Cheerleading advisor position open at Milltown High School. Salary is $1,585. Applications can be obtained and are being accepted at Milltown High, 20202 Main Street, Milltown. Hiring contingent upon fingerprinting -- cost to new hire is $45.

Kids and kittens need room to roam? 38.44 acres with east/north four mountain view. 17.40 acres of timber. 1950 fixer/replace house. Metal shed; well; Milltown schools.

One pair Brazilian Rainbow boas $500.
Canaries, Breeding Red Factors, $1000.
You Do Self Service Doggie Wash. You make the mess and we clean it up!! All washing supplies furnished. 3000 Milltown Road (next to People's Insurance). Appointment not needed.

Free garden manure. We load, you haul, composted horse manure. Call 555-333-2222 for easy directions in Milltown.

I am looking for house sitting job, garage apartment, guest house, or room for rent. Milltown area. Close to the highway, female student.

Pesticide Supervisor. We are seeking an experienced applicator capable of directing other applicators in our pesticide dept. Covering 1000 acres of nursery stock in the Milltown area. Candidates must have supervisory skills, adequate pesticide experience, knowledge of record keeping, calibration experience, safe handling skills, the ability to operate agricultural spray equipment. Company benefits: profit sharing, pay rate from $11 to $13.75.

Volkswagen, 1958 Bug convertible. Black, with black interior and top, all new parts, engine and transmission. $10,000 invested. Sell for $8500 or best offer. Call 555-222-3333/

Ford Mojave 1992, customized with wheel chair lift. Swing away lift with automatic doors, raised roof. 52k miles. Excellent. $15,000.

The voices

Three-year-old child
Sportscaster
Rap artist
Southerner
Person with a cold
News broadcast anchor

Eighty-year old woman
Brooklyn (or Boston) accent
French accent
British or Irish accent
used car sales person
President of the United States

cheerleader
talk show host
televangelist
shy eight-year-old
depressed person
perfume ad voice-over

When you have gone around the circle a time or two, stop and discuss the vocal qualities you needed to take on in order to do each voice. Which was easiest? Which was hardest? Why?

Before You Take the Exam

To test your knowledge and comprehension of elements of delivery, look back over Chapter 14, define the key terms, and answer the following review questions. Go to http://communication.wadsworth.com/jaffe for an interactive list of key terms.

1. Explain the concept of impression management as it relates to speech delivery.
2. Identify at least two ways you can maximize your personal appearance.
3. Define the following types of gestures and tell how they can enhance or hinder speaking effectiveness: emblems, illustrators, regulators, adaptors.
4. Explain the difference between articulation and stress and tell how they are both related to pronunciation.
5. Tell how regional origin, ethnicity, and social status can affect pronunciation.
6. Explain how vocal variation can create impressions -- both positive and negative.
7. Describe how politicians have learned to pay attention to vocal characteristics and other elements of delivery.
8. Differentiate between the confident style and the conversational style.
9. Describe four types of delivery and give the advantages and disadvantages of each.
10. Distinguish between fixed, portable, and lavaliere microphones and tell the advantages and disadvantages of each.
11. Give tips for using microphones successfully.
12. Explain how speaking before a camera requires alterations in appearance and gestures.
13. Give guidelines for using a TelePrompTer.

Sample Questions

1. The concept of impression management uses the analogy of a circus to describe our daily performances. (258)
   ❍ True
   ❍ False
2. In general, choose slightly more formal clothing when you give your speeches. (259)
   ❍ True
   ❍ False
3. Playing with your keys is a self-adaptor that signals your nervousness. (260)
   ❍ True
   ❍ False

4. A well-placed pause gives your audience a chance to think. (265)
   - ❍ True
   - ❍ False

5. Most speeches given in the United States are delivered extemporaneously. (269)
   - ❍ True
   - ❍ False

6. Elements of a confident speaking style include: (266)
   - ❍ vocal variety, fluency, good use of gestures, and maintained eye contact.
   - ❍ calm, slow, soft speaking, with good eye contact and gestures.
   - ❍ slow, measured delivery with good volume and many gestures.
   - ❍ animated, loud delivery characterized by dramatic pausing.

7. Which is NOT a tip for adapting a speech for the camera? (270)
   - ❍ Be more careful to control your facial expressions than when you speak live.
   - ❍ Avoid sweeping gestures and large movements.
   - ❍ Use graceful and fluid movements.
   - ❍ Choose black and white clothing; add pastels for accent color.
   - ❍ Whether male or female, use makeup to camouflage blemishes.

8. According to the text, a candidate who presents himself as an intellectual when he knows he is not one is ____. (260)
   - o putting a spin on his performance.
   - ❍ ethical if his performance is convincing.
   - ❍ being cynical.
   - ❍ insincere.

9. A major reason to avoid adaptors is ________. (260)
   - ❍ they give away the fact that you're nervous.
   - ❍ audiences get distracted by your movements.
   - ❍ they distance you from your listeners, making you look defensive.
   - ❍ they take your attention away from your speech.

10. Eye contact in the United States signals ________ (261)
    - ❍ trustworthiness, honesty, and friendliness.
    - ❍ attentiveness, agreement, and trustworthiness.
    - ❍ honesty, respect, and attentiveness.
    - ❍ friendliness, agreement, and respect.

Answer Bank

1. false
2. true
3. false
4. true
5. true
6. vocal variety, fluency, good use of gestures, and maintained eye contact.
7. Choose black and white clothing; add pastels for accent color.
8. being cynical.
9. they give away the fact that you're nervous.
10. trustworthiness, honesty, and friendliness.

Chapter 15: Telling Narratives

Activity 15.1: Evaluate Narrative Reasoning

Read, then evaluate Michael Henderson's speech, "Lee Johnson's Revenge," on the following page.

- What is Mr. Henderson's general purpose for telling this story?
- Identify his central idea.
- What's the overall "moral to the story"?
- Using the tests for narrative reasoning located in the text on page 282, evaluate Henderson's reasoning.
- How does Henderson use emotion in this speech?
- Which details in the story are particularly vivid?
- Is a narrative more persuasive for this topic than another form of organization might be? (For example, in your opinion does telling Lee Johnson's story argue against racism better than a pro-con or problem-solution or other organizational pattern might?) Why or why not?

Discuss your answers with a small group of your classmates.

SAMPLE NARRATIVE: Lee Johnson's Revenge

Michael Henderson, KBOO radio, Portland, Oregon.

It might, like many another racial incident, have left the community and the victim embittered.

J. Lee Johnson, 34, a black entrepreneur in Lawrence, New Jersey, arrived at his computer company to find racial slurs painted on the walls and a dead bird lying on the doorstep. He had just opened a new company in the neighborhood.

The graffiti contained references to the KKK, a drawing of a painted cross and a slur that read, "No Nigir," As the local paper wrote, "The green spray-painted words were crude and one was even misspelled, but their meaning was clear: blacks are not welcome."

Johnson, whose parents were raised in the South and who knew first hand the racism they had undergone, did not feel welcome. "At first I didn't know what to do," he says. "This was like a cold slap in the face. It knocked a little bit of the wind out of my sails."

But Johnson is tough. His parents had also brought him up never to hate anyone because of their race or religion. "Most people thought I would be in a retaliatory mood," he told me. "But we can't afford to let these things rip our communities."

Local residents and business people rallied round, telling him what had happened was deplorable and didn't reflect the feeling in the neighborhood. "They told me to hang in there." The mayor came by, expressing her horror and the commitment of the community that such actions would not be tolerated. Churches and other community groups, aware that racial incidents although uncommon were not unknown in the area, set up support networks. Johnson's mailbag was "stuffed" with letters from caring people.

Five days after the incident the police had charged the vandal--a ten-year-old boy. "I was floored," Johnson told a racist sensitivity training session at the local Episcopal church. "You really can't say it's the parents' fault. Kids are exposed to hatred and violence on television every day. It's what we are as a community. It's coming out is small children, and it's got to stop."

He decided to reach out to the young man as others had done to him earlier in life, believing that America cannot afford to lose a generation to hatred and bias.

The white youngster had never met a black man. Johnson gave him a tour of his business, meeting blacks, whites, Hispanics, working there. He introduced him to the inside of computers. They sat and talked on the very spot where the boy had left the dead bird.

Today, Johnson says, the boy is doing better at home and school. "He has found a place to channel energies which had gone astray. I like to visualize ten years down the road, what would be his mindset if we don't reach out and show him the beauty of differences in people."

The blotches of paint on the wall that cover over the graffiti still remain. Johnson can't yet afford to paint the building. They are a constant reminder of the past. But the friendship he has built with a young boy who knew no better is a stake in a different future and part of the cure to what he calls the threatening disease of prejudice. A community is the richer for his action.

Activity 15.2: Narrative Purposes in Movies

In oral cultures, members of a community gathered around a fire or in a city plaza area; in an electronic culture, we, too, gather to recount stories, but our stories mainly come from media. Filmed and televised dramas are two sources that tell stories millions in the culture see and share. Like any good narrative, each movie has a general purpose or goal. Make a list of movies you've seen that function in the following ways:

Movies that explain natural, social, or ultimate realities. Examples: Documentaries often explain nature; *Braveheart* and *Gladiator* depict historical happenings (however fictionalized). *The Matrix* suggests an unique answer to the ultimate question "Who are we?"

Movies that provide examples of people who choose admirable behaviors or values or reject and avoid negative behaviors. Examples: *Erin Brockovich*, for all her eccentricities, single-handedly took on a large industry that was polluting the environment. One theme of this story is "individuals can make a difference against injustices." *Wall Street* shows a greedy villain who values money rather than other, more important things.

Movies that contain persuasive messages about controversial cultural issues. Example: Author and screenwriter John Irving accepted an Oscar for the *movie Cider House Rules*. Throughout public appearances during Oscar week, he repeatedly noted that it gave him great pleasure to have been part of a movie that presented a clearly pro-choice message.

Movies that don't depict the here-and-now, but provide a vision of possibilities--what might be, what might happen. Examples: *Contact* or *Independence Day* hint at what might exist "out there."

Movies that exist mainly to entertain. Example: *Analyze This* or *Nodding Hill* are lighthearted films that feature quirky characters in quirky situations.

How do movies represent the United States' culture abroad? Professor Melvin DeFleur (Boston University) says that the sex, violence, and arrogance depicted in American media lead young people around the world to despise Americans. His study, "The Next Generation's Image of Americans: Attitudes and Beliefs by Teenagers in 12 Countries" (2002) concluded that teens were entertained by American media, but they also began to believe that Americans were lewd, drug using, dishonest sex fiends. DeFleur said U.S. media was causing a "culture of hate." Use chapter concepts to explain how the study might be on to something.

Activity 15.3: Create an Interesting Narrative

To make your narrative more interesting, fill in details that bring to life the setting, characters, and plot. These details provide the who, what, where, when, and why of the story.

Character(s): Provide three details about the character(s).

1. ______________________________
2. ______________________________
3. ______________________________

Jot down specific, vivid words and phrases that will bring the character(s) to life. ____________

____

____

Plot: Identify two major details about the plot.

1. What challenge will the character(s) face? ______________________________
2. How will the character(s) meet it? ______________________________

Identify specific, vivid words and phrases about the plot. ______________________________

____

Setting: List three details about the time, place, and situation in which the story takes place.

1. ______________________________
2. ______________________________
3. ______________________________

Identify specific, vivid words and phrases that will help set the scene. ____________

____

____

Moral: Identify the point of the story. ______________________________

____

List vivid words that will drive home the point. ______________________________

____

Identify specific places in the story where you will use constructed dialogue. ____________

____

____

Identify places in the story where a list would enliven the telling. ____________

____

____

Before You Take the Exam

To test your knowledge and comprehension of narrative speaking, reread Chapter 15, define the key terms, and answer the following review questions. Go to http://communication.wadsworth.com/jaffe for an interactive list of key terms.

1. Tell the global importance of narrative speaking.
2. Identify ways that narratives provide information about nature, social institutions, and ultimate questions.
3. Describe how narratives motivate people to choose some values and behaviors and to avoid others.
4. Explain the value of visionary narratives.
5. Tell some forms of entertaining narratives.
6. Give three principles for evaluating narrative reasoning.
7. Give guidelines for choosing the purpose, characters, and plot of a story.
8. Explain how descriptions, dialogue, and lists contribute to vividness of a narrative.
9. Identify the five elements of an exemplum pattern.

Sample Questions

1. Storytelling is more important in oral societies than in literate or electronic cultures. (276)
   - ❍ True
   - ❍ False
2. The purpose of exemplary narratives is to provide information about social realities. (277)
   - ❍ True
   - ❍ False
3. According to the text, Martin Luther King, Jr's, "I Have a Dream" speech is a visionary narrative. (281)
   - ❍ True
   - ❍ False
4. One good place to cluster details is in the setting of a story. (284)
   - ❍ True
   - ❍ False
5. An exemplum is a narrative speech created around a quotation. (286)
   - ❍ True
   - ❍ False

6. Jessica Howard's classroom speech about learning to accept and value her brother's Down Syndrome condition is a good example of a narrative that __________. (279)
   - ❍ explains natural realities.
   - ❍ persuades others to value diversity.
   - ❍ entertains her listeners.
   - ❍ provides a vision of what might be.

7. *Homo narrans* means _______ (276)
   - ❍ humans are storytelling animals.
   - ❍ Human stories explain natural realities.
   - ❍ humans should evaluate stories to see if they merit telling.
   - ❍ human stories are used globally as a form of entertainment.

8. Which of these questions is most important when you ponder the ethics of telling narratives about another person's private life? (282)
   - ❍ Is the story coherent, given the characters involved?
   - ❍ Is the story entertaining?
   - ❍ Do the positive outcomes for the hearers outweigh the negative outcomes for the person?
   - ❍ Does the story model behaviors that the hearers should avoid?

9. The _____ of the story is the challenge the characters face and the way they deal with that challenge. (283)
   - ❍ moral
   - ❍ plot
   - ❍ setting
   - ❍ application
   - ❍ purpose

10. Angela's speech provided details about her own rape, to the discomfort of many in her audience. Which principle was she violating? (284)
    - ❍ Details should be used mainly when she sets the story, describes the key action, and drives home her message.
    - ❍ Details should not reveal more than the audience wants to know.
    - ❍ Too many irrelevant but interesting details can distract and annoy an audience.
    - ❍ Detail should be used to help the audience place themselves psychologically in the scene.

Answer Bank

1. false
2. false
3. true
4. true
5. true
6. persuades others to value diversity.
7. humans are storytelling animals.
8. Do the positive outcomes for the hearers outweigh the negative outcomes for the person?
9. plot
10. Details should not reveal more than the audience wants to know.

CHAPTER 16: INFORMATIVE SPEAKING

Activity 16.1: Topics from the Audience's Perspective

Let's say you're a member of a class in which fellow students give speeches on the following topics. How familiar are you with each subject? In the blank beside each topic, write the letter that corresponds to your level of knowledge.

A = I have no information
B = I have limited information
C = I once knew about it, but I've forgotten most of what I knew
D = my information is probably outdated
E = I have misinformation
F = I am very familiar with the topic

___ how to make chocolate chip cookies

___ how to do laundry

___ how cement curbs along city streets are made

___ how to study in college

___ stages of relationship development

___ educating a chiropractor

___ acupuncture

___ the Nation of Islam

___ macular degeneration (an eye disease)

___ the history of Little League

___ the history of the Negro League

___ vacations in Florida

___ dentistry for pets

___ forest fire fighting techniques

___ climbing Mt. Kilimanjaro

___ ancient empires of Africa

___ how to write a resume

___ acoustic guitars

___ the life of Mother Theresa

___ the effects of folic acid

___ school vouchers

___ the Japanese educational system

Now, go back and select a topic that is very familiar to you. Let's say that the person sitting next to you has chosen that topic for his or her next speech. What specifically could s/he do to inform you and keep your interest?

Select two topics you're somewhat familiar with. What additional information would you like to have about each one?

Which are totally uninteresting? What, if anything, could someone do to make you interested in the subject? What information might you need about the subject?

What advice would you give the person next to you about selecting an informative topic that you'd like to hear about? How can you follow your own advice when you're selecting an informative topic?

Activity 16.2: Evaluate an Informative Speech

Watch a video of an informative student speech. Critique the speech, using guidelines from Activity 4.4 in this workbook which are adapted below.

In the Canon of Invention

- Topic (appropriate? a need to address this topic?)
- Evidence of research (sources cited? credible sources? major points supported with credible data?)
- Sensitivity to audience (meets their needs? deals with possible objections? respectful? etc.)
- Adequate visual aid support?

Comments:

In the Canon of Disposition or Organization

- Introduction (all the parts included? is the intro effective?)
- Body (organizational pattern clear? effectively organized? connectives?)
- Conclusion (all parts here? effective?)

Comments:

In the Canon of Style

- Clear ideas (avoids or defines jargon?)
- Connotative words (effectively used?)
- Avoids demeaning terminology
- Concise
- Interesting (metaphors? repetition? vivid words? etc.)

Comments:

In the Canon of Memory

- Knew major ideas
- Few references to notes

Comments:

In the Canon of Delivery

- Eye contact (inclusive?)
- Appearance (appropriate grooming? clothing? accessories?)
- Voice (effective vocal variety? use of pauses? rate? volume?)
- Time (within limits?)

Comments:

Especially Effective:

Suggestions for Improvement:

Activity 16.3: Evaluate the Audience's Need to Know

The following table lists a number of topics that might be used in informative speeches. How would you interest your classmates in each of these topics? Work with a small group to fill in the blanks.

	Audience's Need to know?	Audience Interest in topic?	Audience Attitude toward it (+ or -)?	Speaker Strategies?
Stalin				
Tips for a successful interview				
Broadway musicals				
Elephant depletion				
Social Security reform				
SUV's effect on the environment				

Before You Take the Exam

To test your knowledge and comprehension of informative speaking, review Chapter 16, be able to define key terms, and answer these review questions. (Follow links to the Jaffe text on the Communication Café web site http://communication.wadsworth.com for an interactive list of key terms.)

1. Explain the importance of information and the equal distribution of information globally.
2. Describe strategies a speaker should use to present new information, present supplemental information, review or update information, and counter misinformation.
3. Give tips for doing demonstrations and providing instructions.
4. Explain how to create effective descriptions of places, objects, and events.
5. Describe characteristics of reports about people and about issues.
6. Explain a two-part pattern you can use in a speech that definesa term or concept.
7. Identify four guidelines for explaining complex or information-dense subjects.
8. Tell seven general tips for making informative speeches more understandable.

Sample Questions

1. Information overload means that there are more than 800 million websites on the Internet. (294)
   - ❍ True
   - ❍ False
2. You should never give a speech about a topic that's already very familiar to your audience. (296)
   - ❍ True
   - ❍ False
3. Audiences tend not to like it when you challenge their misunderstandings. (297)
   - ❍ True
   - ❍ False
4. Timing how long it takes to do a process is important for a speech of explanation. (298)
   - ❍ True
   - ❍ False
5. All "how-to" speeches require visual aids. (298)
   - ❍ True
   - ❍ False

6. Consider your informative speech about a current issue to be a(n) _________ (301-304)
   - ❍ investigative report.
   - ❍ definition of a major social issue.
   - ❍ theoretical explanation of a social problem.
   - ❍ argument advocating change.

7. Think of your explanation speech as a(n) __________ speech. (305-306)
   - ❍ translation
   - ❍ analysis
   - ❍ functional
   - ❍ instructional

8. Doing an obstacle analysis of your audience means that you _____ . (307)
   - ❍ choose your vocabulary carefully.
   - ❍ identify those sections of the speech that will probably be hard for listeners to understand.
   - ❍ use a repetitive style to present your major points.
   - ❍ compare the known to the unknown.

9. Demonstrations answer your listeners' question: __________ ? (298)
   - ❍ What is that?
   - ❍ How does that work?
   - ❍ Why?
   - ❍ How do you do that?

10. When your listeners have forgotten some of what they knew about a subject, your best strategy is to _____ . (296)
    - ❍ counter their misconceptions.
    - ❍ approach the subject from different angles.
    - ❍ go over the basic facts again.
    - ❍ provide information about just one aspect of the topic.

Answer Bank

1. false
2. false
3. true
4. false
5. false
6. investigative report
7. translation
8. identify those sections of the speech that will probably be hard for listeners to understand.
9. How do you do that?
10. approach the subject from different angles.

CHAPTER 17: PERSUASIVE SPEAKING

Activity 17.1: Finding a Topic You Care About

Find a topic that is important enough to you that you could speak out about it. Use the suggestions below as you brainstorm for a topic. Then select one and create a persuasive speech about it.

The stupidest law on the books is

The environmental issue that most concerns me is

I worry that ____________________ will happen the future, but we could prevent this if we just

____ now.

We should all help our neighbors by

National attitudes need to change about

The most disgusting form of entertainment is

There outta be a law against

This college or university would be better if

I wish my friends would

Our society is too complacent about

Our society is overly concerned about

I wish politicians would

Sports should be reformed by

Choose one topic and identify a claim of fact, a claim of value, and a claim of policy for it.

Activity 17.2: Setting Criteria (Value Claims)

Think of criteria as the ideas you have formed about what's most desirable or ideal, given a specific object, relationship, activity, and so on. Criteria are the means (often unstated) that we use to form and argue value claims.

List four qualities you look for in your personal car? (Put another way, what criteria do you personally use to judge whether or not a particular model is good overall and whether or not it's right for you?)

1.
2.
3.
4.

Which make or model of car best fulfills these criteria? ______________________________

List four things you want out of a sport or recreational activity? (Put another way, what criteria do you personally look for when you decide whether or not to try a new activity?)

1.
2.
3.
4.

Which sport or recreation best fulfills your criteria? ______________________________

List four characteristics of a good movie? (Put another way, what does a movie need to have in order for you to rent the video or spend $8.00 [or the going rate] on a ticket?)

1.
2.
3.
4.

Which genre of movies or what specific movies best fulfill your criteria? ____________________

Identify five qualities you look for in a close friend [or someone you'd consider for a lifetime partnership]? (Or ask yourself the criteria you personally use to judge whether or not to spend time forming a relationship [maybe even a permanent one] with an individual?)

1.
2.
3.
4.
5.

Identify two people who fulfill your criteria: ______________________________

Activity 17.3: Value Clashes

When different people have divergent, but unstated criteria for their evaluations of what's good, what's significant, or what's moral, they often clash. Some value differences are minor, others are major--leading to wars. This activity will help you better understand value claims.

Using the topics in Activity 17.2, make a value claim that goes with each general topic. Use words like "great" or "best" in your claim. [e.g. "'Model X' is the best car on the road." Or "'Movie A' was an excellent movie."]

Now find someone in the class who has a very different claim from yours. Sit down together, read your claims to one another, and start to argue.

[e.g. you:	*Movie A was an excellent movie*
other:	*I thought it was awful.*
You:	*Awful? What do you mean awful?*
Other	*You know, just awful!"*

After awhile, ask your partner to specify the criteria s/he's using. Discuss likenesses and differences in your criteria. Discuss why you could or why you probably shouldn't go to the movies together.

Now create a scenario about a more significant topic:

Make a list of criteria for a relational partner or spouse. Have your classmate create very different--even opposite--criteria. (e.g. if you list *fun-loving,* your classmate lists *serious minded.* If you list *daring and adventuresome,* your classmate says *stable and predictable.*) Let the classmate's list represent the "parent" figure.

The scenario is this:

- One of you acts the role of a person who has just brought his or her ideal soul mate home to meet the family. The soul mate has just gone into the bathroom, and you are alone with your parent. You say, "Isn't this the most wonderful person you've ever seen?"
- The other person plays the role of the parent.

Discuss the kind of clash that different criteria create in situations like this.

To understand clashes on a regional or national level, return to Figure 3.1 in Chapter 3 in the text. Identify the criteria that a developer might set for wise use of land. Then identify the criteria the environmentalist might use.

Before You Take the Exam

To test your knowledge and comprehension of persuasive reasoning methods, review Chapter 17, be able to define key terms, and answer these review questions. Go to http://communication.wadsworth.com/jaffe for an interactive list of key terms.

1. Give examples of persuasion in Rome, the Soviet Union, Athabaskan culture, and in international negotiations.
2. Explain three types of factual claims and give examples for each.
3. Explain what a value claim is and give examples; tell how we judge value claims.
4. Define policy claim and describe two types of policy claims.
5. Show how fact, value, and policy claims can all be made about the same subject.
6. Describe an unconvinced audience and give guidelines for persuading them.
7. Distinguish between an unmotivated and an unfocused audience and give strategies for persuading each type.
8. Explain the theory of cognitive dissonance and describe how dissonance can be a motivator for change in an inconsistent person.
9. Tell strategies for speaking to an audience whose beliefs and actions are consistent with one another.
10. Explain the importance of criteria to value claims.
11. Draw an attitude scale.
12. Describe guidelines for speaking to audiences whose attitudes are positive, neutral, apathetic, mildly negative, and hostile.
13. Explain the problem-solution pattern and tell how its use in informative speeches differs from its persuasive use.
14. Give another name for the direct method pattern.
15. Describe and give examples of the direct method pattern.
16. Describe and give examples of the comparative advantages pattern.
17. Describe and give examples of the criteria satisfaction pattern.
18. Describe and give examples of the negative method pattern.
19. List and explain five elements of Monroe's Motivated Sequence.

Sample Questions

1. "Angels exist" is a claim of fact. (318)
   - ❍ True
   - ❍ False

2. "Consumers should stop using their credit cards so much" is an argument against the status quo. (319)
   - ❍ True
   - ❍ False

3. Unmotivated audiences fail to act out of apathy. (322)
   - ❍ True
   - ❍ False

4. The "need" step is unique to Monroe's Motivated Sequence; no other pattern has a comparable element. (328)
   - ❍ True
   - ❍ False

5. An apathetic audience generally has a neutral attitude toward a topic. (325)
   - ❍ True
   - ❍ False

6. When dealing with a hostile audience, a speaker should _____ (326)
   2. kindly, but directly, rebuke them for their attitude.
   3. stop speaking and leave the stage when they get too annoying.
   4. emphasize areas of common ground between himself and his listeners.
   5. appeal to their emotions.

7. Which pattern do these points fall into? College U is better than College U2 because it is located in a nicer area; it has more nationally known faculty members; and it has better financial aid packages. (330)
   - ❍ comparative advantages
   - ❍ criteria satisfaction
   - ❍ direct method
   - ❍ negative method

8. A problem-solution pattern, used to organize a persuasive speech, differs from one used to organize an informative speech in the following way: (327)
   - ❍ It is not as effective when used to organize an informative speech.
   - ❍ An informative speaker presents possible solutions, without advocating for any.
   - ❍ A persuasive speaker presents only one solution, the one she advocates.
   - ❍ There is no difference between the informative and persuasive speeches.

9. International speakers are adopting Western methods of reasoning for all these reasons EXCEPT ______ (316)
   - ❍ many of their leaders were educated in American universities.
   - ❍ they realize that Western rhetoric is superior to other rhetorics.
   - ❍ they are involved in negotiations where these forms are appropriate.
   - ❍ they can use these forms to communicate their nation's viewpoints more effectively.

10. Dissonance theory argues that ________ . (323)

   - most people experience psychological discomfort when their beliefs and their actions are consistent.
   - psychological balance is not really possible
   - most people are comfortable with the challenges that inconsistency brings.
   - Inconsistency is one of the best motivators for change.

Answer Bank

1. true
2. true
3. true
4. false
5. true
6. emphasize areas of common ground between himself and his listeners.
7. comparative advantages
8. The persuasive speaker presents only one solution, the one she advocates.
9. they realize that Western rhetoric is superior to other rhetorics.
10. Inconsistency is one of the best motivators for change

CHAPTER 18: PERSUASIVE REASONING METHODS

Activity 18.1: Reasoning by Analogy

Reread, then evaluate Don Smith's argument in "Mere Law, Mere Medicine, Mere Rhetoric," found in Activity 1.2 in this workbook. His major form of reasoning is by analogy. Analyze his speech, using the following guidelines.

What is Smith's claim?

His central idea?

Is he basically targeting beliefs? Actions? Values? Attitudes?

What analogies does he use?

Are these analogies convincing to you?

How does Smith use pathos?

How is his credibility established?

What part of his argument is most effective?

What part is least convincing to you?

Activity 18.2: Evaluating Logos, Pathos, and Ethos

Read this student persuasive speech, stopping to answer the questions that appear throughout.

Unnecessary Institutionalization of Teens,

Student speech by Kimber Weaver, Oregon State University

Cynthia Parker, 13 years old, was an overly hyperactive child. She took mild medication to help her pay attention in school. This was ineffective; her parents could not keep up with her. In 1985 she was admitted to a private psychiatric hospital.

We might feel sympathetic to Cynthia's worn out parents, but is this reason enough to turn her over to strangers who fill her full of drugs and think she's crazy?

Unfortunately, according to May 1990 *Ladies' Home Journal*, Cynthia's case is not unique. Private institutions are becoming a fad among frustrated parents who can afford them. Between 1971, about the time many of us were born, and 1985, admissions jumped from 7000 to 99,000 patients. That is more than 4 times the number of undergraduates at Oregon State University.

Sadly, most are fairly normal teens whose major offenses are talking back, messy rooms, or less-than-straight A grade point averages. This is not right. Private institutions are hurting American youth.

This topic intrigued me because I am interested in psychiatry and the service it provides to society, and I have read many articles and seen shows on the injustices suffered by teens in mental wards.

Today, I will explain the causes and propose some solutions to the problem of unnecessary institutionalization of teens.

- *Kimber uses the narrative of Cynthia Parker throughout her speech. This story is an extended example. As you continue to read, apply the tests for examples to Cynthia's story.*
- *How effectively does Kimber establish her credibility on this topic here in the introduction?*

Many factors contribute to the problem of teens being institutionalized in such alarming numbers. Causes starts with publicity from the hospitals themselves. They engage in intensive campaigns using newspapers, radio, TV, magazines, even billboards. For instance, one ad shows a boy dressed in a leather jacket, wearing handcuffs, with the caption, "Don't wait until you get a call from the police to get help for your teenager."

This type of ad combined with severe drug and suicide problems among youth make parents even more suspicious of their child's actions. According to Dr. Paul Fink, past president of the American Psychiatric Association, "Bad conduct is not a reason to put someone in the hospital. Eighty to ninety percent of what they are calling conduct disorder could be treated outside."

Another cause is stated by Dr. Thomas S. Szasz in Bruce Ennis' book, *Prisoners of Psychiatry*, "Many psychiatrists are now ready to classify anyone and everyone as mentally sick and anything and everything as psychiatric treatment."

- *So far, Kimber has provided evidence to explain the problem's causes. Are her sources trustworthy?*
- *Apply the tests for causal reasoning to her argument here. Does she convince you that these things the major causes?*
- *Look for additional causes mentioned later in her speech.*

The problem is not only in the number being treated, it is also in the kind of treatment given. Many use a rewards/ punishment system to control patients. For example, if the patient follows trivial rules, she gets a good meal or gets to wear street clothes instead of pajamas. Once, when Cynthia was "uncontrollable," attendants rolled her in a gym mat and tied it up. "I got rope marks all the way down my body," Cynthia remembers.

Ira Schwartz, Director of the University of Michigan Center for the Study of Youth Policy, says, "These techniques are demeaning and dehumanizing. They adversely affect self-esteem and make kids bitter and angry."

Drugs are also used routinely. Cynthia had a "conduct disorder;" she testifies, "They put me on drugs right away. They told me I was depressed and suicidal. That really threw me."

"We have the power, with electroshock and neuroleptic drugs like thorazine, to take away people's minds. The frightening thing is that we use it," states Maryland psychiatrist, Peter Breggin.

- *How does Kimber use emotional appeals in this section?*
- *Evaluate her use of emotions. Do her appeals to emotions give you a "good reason" to believe?*

Questions arise: what gives these psychiatrists the power to manipulate minds, and what motivates their desire?

Sadly enough, the law gives psychiatrists the power. The law allows mental health experts to define normal and abnormal behavior. The law allows them to decide treatment for various behavioral problems. Teens have no say in whether they belong there, how they should be treated, or when they should be released. A 1979 Supreme Court decision ruled it constitutional to deny minors the right to have a review of their admission in court, as long as the psychiatrist at the institution believes the child should be hospitalized.

Many contend that doctors diagnose out of greed. The cost of treatment in private hospitals may reach $27,000 per month. Hospitals must keep beds full. Cynthia is a good example of how money makes a difference. After three months, Cynthia was released, even though she exhibited strong mood swings and suicidal fantasies. Her doctors claimed she was doing better. A few days later, she tried to cut her wrists. Coincidentally, this "improvement" occurred only after her father informed the hospital that his insurance was running out.

- *How does Kimber's use of language contribute to her argument? Reread this section and identify connotative words that indicate her bias about her topic.*
- *How's she doing so far in establishing her credibility?*
- *In your opinion, has she adequately established the significance of the problem? Why or why not?*

As you can see, this is a serious problem; something needs to be done. No one should be treated this way. Some solutions to this problem are: publicity, better law enforcement, more power to patient advocates, and more outpatient care.

We need more publicity to let the public know what goes on in mental wards. Many are unaware that there is a problem. This may make parents think before they admit their child to an institution.

More law enforcement is needed. Many psychiatrists have abused their authority. Strong legislative guidelines are needed. We can support lawmakers' efforts to provide this legislation.

More patient advocates would make this process more efficient. Patient advocates are outsiders to the hospital who come in and watch over the ward procedures. They could be very useful in helping those who are falsely diagnosed, that is, if the law gives them more power to override the psychiatrists' decisions.

Finally, we need more outpatient care. Sally Zinman, ex-patient, says, "We need to help people before they get caught up in the mental-health care system." With multiple problems facing us today, we need more places where adults and teens can go to have someone help them work through problems, not create more. Even we can help by being aware and by helping friends and families go through hard times. People need to believe that mental hospitals are not the answer.

- *She basically argues that these solutions will cure the problem. Do you agree?*
- *What's her basic goal in this speech? In other words, how would she complete this sentence, "As a result of my speech, my audience will . . . "?*

- *Does she accomplish her goal?*

Unnecessary institutionalization of teens is a growing problem in our nation. We have looked at the problem and some proposed solutions. You and I can have a part in those solutions by being aware of the problem and supporting stronger legislation to control mental hospitals. As for Cynthia, I guess you could say she is lucky; she made it out of the system, but the experience will always haunt her.

- *Overall, how would you judge the reasoning in this speech?*

Before You Take the Exam

To test your knowledge and comprehension of persuasive reasoning methods, review Chapter 18, be able to define key terms, and answer these review questions. Go to http://communication.wadsworth.com/jaffe for an interactive list of key terms.

1. Draw and explain the elements in Toulmin's model of reasoning.
2. Define logos.
3. Distinguish between literal and figurative analogies and give examples for each.
4. Tell how to test analogies.
5. Summarize cultural influences on reasoning patterns.
6. Explain inductive reasoning and give an example.
7. Give three tests for inductive reasoning.
8. Explain deductive reasoning and illustrate by giving a syllogism of your own.
9. Explain the relationship between inductive and deductive reasoning.
10. Identify two major tests for deductive reasoning.
11. Define causal reasoning and tell how to test it.
12. Explain the following reasoning fallacies and give examples for each: unsupported assertion, *ad populum, ad hominem,* false analogy, *post hoc,* overgeneralization, red herring, false dichotomy.
13. Define pathos.
14. Distinguish between appeals to positive emotions and appeals to negative emotions.

15. Identify the five levels in Maslow's heirarchy of needs, and give examples of a topic related to each need.

16. Explain four factors that make motivations complex, rather than simple.

17. Explain ways to test emotional appeals.

18. Define ethos.

19. List and explain four elements of ethos.

20. Give examples of how expectations about composure vary cross culturally.

21. Define invitational rhetoric.

22. Explain three principles of invitational rhetoric.

23. Describe the two forms of invitational rhetoric.

Sample Questions

1. A warrant is a justification. (339)
   - ❍ True
   - ❍ False

2. Support for the warrant is called "backing." (339)
   - ❍ True
   - ❍ False

3. "This policy worked in Idaho; we should try it in Alabama" is an example of reasoning by an analogy. (343)
   - ❍ True
   - ❍ False

4. "We all know that boxing is a dumb sport" is an example of the *ad hominem* fallacy. (347)
   - ❍ True
   - ❍ False

5. One research study showed that women in science use inductive, deductive, and causal reasoning very differently from men. (347)
   - ❍ True
   - ❍ False

6. The "Medi-scare" strategy used in political debates is an example of reasoning by __ (350)
   - ❍ pathos.
   - ❍ mixed motives.
   - ❍ invitational rhetoric.
   - ❍ appeals to needs.

7. "I believe that speaker because she really seems concerned about me" is a way of saying that she is ____ (354)

   - demonstrating good sense.
   - exhibiting good character.
   - expressing goodwill.
   - showing dynamism.

8. What kind of car will Judd buy? Why, a Chrysler, of course. The company makes dependable cars. This is an example of ______ reasoning. (344-345)
   - fallacious.
   - inductive.
   - deductive.
   - causal.

9. A way of deliberating about issues that focuses less on winning the argument than on understanding perspectives is __________. (355)

   - Toulmin's model of reasoning.
   - Aristotle's three types of proof: *logos, pathos,* and *ethos.*
   - invitational rhetoric.
   - identifying one's own and the other's fallacious reasoning.

10. Judd reasons that *a majority* of Chrysler cars are dependable. The term "a majority" is a(n) __________. (339)
    - claim.
    - warrant.
    - piece of data or evidence.
    - qualifier.

Answer Bank

1. true
2. true
3. true
4. false
5. false
6. pathos.
7. expressing goodwill.
8. deductive.
9. invitational rhetoric.
10. qualifier.

PART II

SPEECH ASSIGNMENT OPTIONS, EXAMPLES, AND FORMS

Current Issue Speech
Evaluation Form: Current Issue Speech

Persuasive Speech
Sample Outline (Persuasive Speech to Actuate): Organ Donation, by Danielle Schutz
Evaluation Form: Persuasive Speech (General Form)
Evaluation Form: Persuasive Speech (Monroe's Motivated Sequence)

Panel Discussion: A Current Controversial or Problematic Issue
Group Presentation: Movie Reality vs. Print Reality
Evaluation Form: Panel Discussion or Group Presentation

Below you'll find a list of criteria that speech instructors throughout the country routinely distribute. These guidelines will help you understand typical grading requirements.

Adapted from guidelines of the National Communication Association

CRITERIA FOR EVALUATING SPEECHES

The average speech (grade "C") should meet these criteria:

--Conform to the kind of speech assigned (informative, persuasive, etc.)
--Be original.
--Be appropriate to the audience.
--Meet time requirements (assigned date, time limits).
--Fulfill the assignment's requirements such as use of a visual aid.
--Have an identifiable introduction, body, and conclusion.
--Have a clear central idea.
--Be reasonably direct and competent in delivery (extemporaneous, NOT read).
--Be free of errors in grammar, pronunciation, and word usage.
--Use at least three sources (where required).

The above average speech (grade "B") should also:

--Deal with a challenging topic, adapted to the audience.
--Fulfill all the major requirements of introduction and conclusion.
--Demonstrate research through use of at least 5 sources, clearly identified in the speech.
--Create and sustain attention.
--Exhibit proficient use of connectives such as transitions.
--Be direct and competent in style and delivery.

The superior speech (grade "A") should also:

--Genuinely contribute to the knowledge and beliefs of the audience.
--Demonstrate greater research (7 sources).
--Use vivid language, maintaining special interest.
--Be delivered extemporaneously in a commendable manner.

The below average speech (grade "D" or "F") is seriously deficient in the criteria required for the "C" speech.

D = unrehearsed, biased, or unsupported opinions.
F = fabricated evidence, distorted evidence, plagiarized.

SPEECH ASSIGNMENT: Telling a Modern Legend

Time: 1 1/2 to 3 minutes

Description: Introduce yourself by telling a legend that's been handed down from either your *family* or from a *significant group* to which you belong such as your sports team, living group, religious group, club, or place of work. You may choose one of the oral stories from exercise 4, page 18 of the text. The speech consists of two parts:

- **Part 1** is composed of the story itself, and will take most of the time of the speech.
- **Part 2** identifies the main lesson of the story in which you reveal some of your personal traits or the values you believe are important.

Skills

- Select an story appropriate to the assignment and time limitations.
- Identify the point of the story and link that point to yourself.
- Introduce and conclude the story in an interesting manner.
- Survive!!

Guidelines

1. Select an appropriate legend. Consider the complexity of the story. Can it be told within the short time period? Does your audience have enough background knowledge so the story will make sense to them? What does the story reveal about your personality?

2. List the events of the story in chronological order. Include relevant details the audience needs in order to understand your narrative. After your main events are in order, edit out irrelevant details that do not contribute to the point of the story.

3. Write out the point of the story and the characteristics it reveals about your family or group. Link those characteristics to yourself.

4. Plan an opening statement that draws the audience's attention to your topic. DO NOT say, "I'm gonna tell a story about my grandma." Here are a few suggestions:

    - Start your story with a specific time and place. "When my grandmother was 12 years old, she sailed to the United States alone."

    - Start with a short quotation that tells the moral of your story. "They say that only the good die young; one of my soccer team's heroes proves that saying."

5. Write key <u>words</u> on a note card so that you can jog your memory during your speech. Do not write out the speech word-for-word. Do not try to memorize the speech.

6. Rehearse the main ideas of the speech. Select the exact wording only as you rehearse. Your speech should sound just a little bit different each time.

SAMPLE SPEECH: A Modern Legend (self-introduction)

by Derek Reamy, Loyola University, Maryland

I'm from the South; and if you come from the South, or know anything about the South, you'll know how important good cooking is to a Southerner. Eating meals together is a tradition in my family. Every holiday of my childhood was spent over a meal at my grandparents' home, enjoying my grandmother's cooking. Hand in hand with the meal was storytelling--my grandfather being the center of storytelling attention. He told stories about everything: the family murders, people in the neighborhood, his childhood, and even stories about food!

One story I remember in particular was one he told about some of his experiences as a child during the Great Depression. after our meal was finished, he'd push back his chair, look at me, and begin.

"Boy," he'd say, "let me tell you 'bout when I was comin' up. You think you got it hard now, but I say you all got it easy. When I was a boy--during the Depression--we didn't have non of this here fancy food. Just potatoes!

Baked potatoes,

boiled potatoes,

creamed potatoes,

mashed potatoes,

potato salad,

potato soup . . .

"Biscuits too, if we was lucky. Nothin' better than momma's warm biscuits with a bit of butter. Course, no one had butter then,. But IF you did, you gave thanks. You gave thanks to the good Lord no matter what ya had," he'd tell me.

"Give thanks," he commanded me throughout my life, and accompanying this advice was the example of his life lived in thanks. His thankfulness never stopped when the meal was finished and the food cleared away. Instead, he was grateful throughout all aspects of his life. My grandfather's life--and this story he tells--illustrates for me what it is to be thankful. Through his example, I have learned to be thankful for what I am given.

EVALUATION FORM: Telling a Modern Legend

Time: 1 1/2 to 3 minutes

Name ______________________________ Time ________

Speech Content

___ Story appropriate to the audience and assignment

___ Interesting opening statement

___ Understandable order of events

___ Edited; all material relevant

___ Point of story is clear

___ Point is linked to speaker

Delivery

(Your instructor will describe your behaviors such as eye contact, posture and gestures, use of your voice.)

Memory

_____ Obviously well rehearsed

_____ Use of one note card only; no complete sentences

Grade _____

SPEECH ASSIGNMENT: Birth Date Speech

Time: 1 to 1 1/2 minutes

Description: In this brief self-introduction use something that happened on the day, week, or month of your birthday to reveal important information about yourself.

Skills

- Research in the periodicals section of the library.
- Identification of an important personal characteristic or value.
- Success in extemporaneous delivery

Guidelines

1. Go to the periodicals section of the library and find a newspaper or magazine published on your birthday, or birth week or month. For instance, find a *New York Times* published on the exact date of your birth. Or look at a *Rolling Stone* magazine published fifteen years ago in your birth month. Browse until you find an interesting article, advertisement, sports feature, movie review, television guide, etc.

2. Use something from this article or feature to tell about one of your significant personal characteristics.

3. Prepare a short speech that identifies your birth date, describes the contents of the article or feature, and explains the personal characteristic that made this article or feature significant to you.

4. Write key words on note cards to use in your delivery.

   Point A: Key words from your introductory statement.

   Point B: Key words that describe your selected feature.

   Point C: Key words that describe your personal characteristic.

Examples:

Margo found an advertisement that featured a woman stating, "The way to a man's heart is through his stomach." She contrasted the slogan to her own views of gender relationships.

Micah was born on the day President Ronald Reagan was shot by a would-be assassin. He used this event to tell of his interest in political science.

Other students have used sporting events, television programs, dance reviews, political news, merchandise prices, and so on to introduce themselves.

SAMPLE SPEECH: Birth Date (self-introduction)

Bob Pettit, Oregon State University

Bob skimmed a newspaper from the day he was born. Since no single article "leaped out" as significant, he combined elements of several to reveal some of the experiences that led him to return to college after many years.

I read the Oregonian from the day of my birth--November 28, 1952--and I was struck by how much the world has grown right along with me.

The news was unspectacular that day--a collage of things, many foreshadowing events yet to come--growing pains, if you will, of a world struggling to figure out how it's really done. How to live without war and racism. How to know and be our-selves. How to confront the dishonesty of governments to their people and of people to themselves.

The tantrum of war was evident. The Korean peace talks had bogged down. Ho Chi Min wanted a truce with France. Americans still gloated in self satisfaction at having won the "Big One." The Cold War was chilly indeed. McCarthyism was in full swing.

A front page headline told of a busload of "Negro" soldiers in South Carolina who were sentenced to jail and fined $1570, because one of them sat next to a white girl. This article was countered by another headline--the U. S. Attorney General's call for the end of racial segregation in the public schools.

Reading that paper also struck me by what was not there.

There was nothing about me. It would have been nice to have seen some-thing, you know, nothing much really, maybe a little box in the corner of the front page, "Bob Pettit has arrived." But no, nothing was mentioned. Nothing that really gave a clue to my future nature--my likes and dislikes, the essence of me. There should have been something about rattlesnakes and sawmills, cab driving and rock and roll, about world travel, alcohol, Alcoholic Anonymous, but there was none of it, these growing pains yet to come, unforeseen.

And this reinforces my belief that in order to grow there must be a place from which to grow; that part of growing up is--well, growing up. And that we all have had the need to let out a whoop and a yell.

EVALUATION FORM: Birth Date Speech

Time: 1 to 1 1/2 minutes

Name ______________________________________Time __________

Speech Content

_____ Effective introductory statement

_____ Description of research item(s)

_____ Explanation of personal characteristic

Delivery

(Your instructor will describe your behaviors such as eye contact, posture and gestures, use of your voice.)

Memory

_____ Obviously well rehearsed

_____ Use of one note card only; no complete sentences

Grade _____

SPEECH ASSIGNMENT: Single Point Speech

Time: 2 to 3 minutes

Description: In a single point speech, you present only one major idea and develop it with several pieces of supporting information.

Skills:

- Ability to state a major idea.
- Ability to state and explain reasons that support the idea.
- Interesting introduction
- Memorable conclusion
- Selection of appropriate language
- Extemporaneous delivery

Guidelines:

1. Select one major idea that you can support with several reasons. Suggestions: Vacations are important. Volunteering to coach in the Special Olympics enriched my life. There are three good reasons NOT to cohabitate before marriage.

2. Provide reasons to support your major idea. Use such materials as examples, facts, and statistics to explain your reasons for making that statement. You may have to do library research, interview a knowledgeable person, draw from your own experiences, or use electronically stored data as you gather you supporting materials.

3. Plan a brief introduction to orient your audience to your topic.

4. Think the speech through to a concluding statement.

5. Rehearse the speech. Don't memorize exact wording; instead, learn only the major ideas and the relationship between them. Put key words on note cards to use as you speak.

SAMPLE SPEECH: Come Watch Lacrosse

by Andres Lucero, St. John's University, New York

Introduction Have you ever sat and watched a long, boring baseball game? You all know the deal: ball . . . strike . . . ball. . . strike. . . ten minutes later, a pop up. Well, if you've endured such "entertainment," and agree that there might be more exciting things to do with your time, you should try watching a sport created by Native Americans--one that is fast and exciting, hard hitting, and very strategic. A sport like lacrosse. As you may know, I play lacrosse for the university.

[Single point] Today, I will explain why you should watch a lacrosse game.

First Reason Lacrosse is fast and exciting. In fact, it's called the fastest sport in the world, because the clock runs constantly and only stops for a few seconds when the ball goes out of bounds. Unlike baseball or football, players never have time to rest. For that reason, there are many substitutions during the game. Since there is always action on the field, there is never a boring moment. Watching lacrosse is similar to watching a long rally in a tennis match, yet the game itself is as hard hitting as football.

Second Reason Lacrosse is a very physical game. Since it's a contact sport, not surprisingly, there is lots of right contact. If I'm not careful, I can be seriously injured. I know this from experience. In my first month of college play, I had a painful introduction to Division I lacrosse. On too many occasions, I found myself lying flat on my back, with nothing but sky in view. I discovered that many lacrosse players set up a kill and look to just cream a guy. However, a player doesn't have to be roughed up. Some players--myself included--try to use strategy to outsmart the opponent.

Third Reason Good players and good teams do not just go out and run around the field, they plan what they will do; then they execute their plan. When you watch a game, you can see how the entire team works together to make goals. Most of the finesse teams, those who concentrate on strategy, win more often than those who look for ways to injure their opponents.

Conclusion You now have three good reasons to watch a lacrosse game--it is a fast, hard-hitting sport that requires much strategy to win. So the next time you find yourself sitting in front of the TV watching a ball . . . then a strike . . . then a ball. . . then ten minutes later, a pop up, get up and go experience a lacrosse game first hand!

EVALUATION FORM: Single Point Speech

Time: 2 to 3 minutes

Name ______________________________Time ________

Speech Content

___ Gains attention in introduction

___ Single point clearly stated

___ Reasons clearly stated

___ Each reason explained

___ Memorable concluding statement

___ Appropriate language

Delivery

(Your instructor will describe your behaviors such as eye contact, posture and gestures, use of your voice.)

Memory

___ Evidence of practice

___ Minimal use of note cards

Grade ____

SELF-EVALUATION FORM

Name ___________________________ Speech ____________________

Write B (before), D (during) or A (after) if you experienced any of these reactions as you presented your speech.

Physical Symptoms

____ Heart pounding
____ Constriction of throat
____ Voice not normal? How? ___________
____ Trembling? Where? _______________
____ Feeling too warm, face flushed, blushing
____ Dry mouth
____ Increased perspiration
____ "Butterflies" in the stomach
____ Other __________________________

Physical Preparation

____ Got a good night's sleep
____ Limited my caffeine
____ Consciously relaxed
____ Ate sensibly

Mental Preparation

____ Knew physical symptoms were normal
____ Took preparation and rehearsal time
____ Assumed my audience was positive
____ Assured myself I would do OK
____ Thought how interesting my topic was
____ Focused on my personal strengths
____ Kept the speech in perspective
____ Visualized myself giving a great speech

1. I noticed that my listeners . . . .

2. Other speakers . . .

3. My goals for this speech were . . .

4. In this speech, my strengths and weaknesses were . . .

5. My instructor can help me improve by . . .

SPEECH ASSIGNMENT: A Tribute

Time: 2 to 3 minutes

Definition: A tribute is a special kind of ceremonial speech that praises the characteristics of people who exemplify important traits that make society better.

Skills

- Identify an important cultural belief, value, attitude, or behavior.
- Identify a person or who embodies that cultural resource.
- Prepare a speech that praises the chosen trait.
- Prepare an introduction and conclusion for your speech.

Guidelines

1. Choose a worthy subject, contemporary or historical, whose characteristics and values are worthy of admiration. Heroes--famous or lesser known--come from many fields such as medicine, education, politics, and religion.

2. Arrange your speech into an introduction, body, and conclusion as the following guidelines explain:

3. Introduce your subject by planning an interesting opening line. For example, instead of saying, "Today I am going to talk about Bill Gates who is an important American," one student stated the number of people employed at Microsoft, people who depend on Mr. Gates' creativity for their livelihood. Another began his tribute to the late dancer Martha Graham with a quotation from a New York Times' review which praised the creativity and energy Ms. Graham brought to the world of dance. After your opening statement, provide enough information for the audience to understand who your subject is and why she or he deserves praise.

4. The body of your speech reveals worthy characteristics including some or all of these elements:
   - Background: parentage, hardships, or ethnic roots, and so on.
   - Education: educational background, whether positive or negative.
   - Achievements: character traits in three areas: personality (such as friendliness or curiosity), physical attributes (such as speed or endurance), and characteristics of the spirit (such as courage or perseverance). Use examples that demonstrate your points. Summarize the subject's lasting achievements or enduring legacy.

5. Conclusion. Think your speech through to the very end. Conclude with a summary of the major values embodied in the life of your character, values that other people can emulate. Finish, as you began, with a memorable statement.

SAMPLE SPEECH: A Tribute to the Dog

George Graham Vest (1830-1904)

Tributes can focus on ideas such as "justice" or "liberty" as well as animals who exhibit valued traits. This speech praises a dog. The speaker, a lawyer in a small Missouri town, represented one man who sued another for killing his dog. This is Vest's summation speech to the jury. (As you might guess, his client won the case.) Vest went on to become United States senator from Missouri from 1879-1903.

This speech is more than 100 years old. As you read through it, notice the changes in language that have occurred in the century. For one thing, Vest uses "he" to mean people in general. In addition, compare the lawyer's formal style to the informality you'll find in the electronic drums speech found at the end of Chapter 13 in your text.

GENTLEMEN OF THE JURY: The best friend a man has in the world may turn against him and become his enemy. His son or daughter that he has reared with loving care may prove ungrateful. Those who are nearest and dearest to us, those whom we trust with our happiness and our good name may become traitors to their faith. The money that a man has, he may lose. It flies away from him, perhaps when he needs it most. A man's reputation may be sacrificed in a moment of ill-considered action. The people who are prone to fall on their knees to do us honor when success is with us, may be the first to throw the stone of malice when failure settles its cloud upon our heads.

The one absolutely unselfish friend that man can have in this selfish world, the one that never deserts him, the one that never proves ungrateful or treacherous is his dog. A man's dog stands by him in prosperity and in poverty, in health and in sickness. He will sleep on the cold ground, where the wintry winds blow and the snow drives fiercely, if only he may be near his master's side. He will kiss the hand that has no food to offer; he will lick the wounds and sores that come in encounter with the roughness of the world. He guards the sleep of his pauper master as if he were a prince. When all other friends desert, he remains. When riches take wings, and reputation falls to pieces, he is as constant in his love as the sun in its journey through the heavens.

If fortune drives the master forth an outcast in the world, friendless and homeless, the faithful dog asks no higher privilege than that of accompanying him, to guard him against danger, to fight against his enemies. And when the last scene of all comes, and death takes his master in its embrace and his body is laid away in the cold ground, no matter if all other friends pursue their way, there by the graveside will the noble dog be found, his head between his paws, his eyes sad, but open in alert watchfulness, faithful and true even in death.

Discussion Questions

1. What characteristics of the dog does Vest praise? What would our society be like if more people behaved as Vest argues a dog behaves?

2. Do you know of a person who would be a good speech subject because he or she embodies the characteristics that Vest praises here?

EVALUATION FORM: A Tribute

Name ____________________________________ Time __________ (2 to 3 minutes)

Speech Content

____ Creative opening

____ Subject introduced clearly

____ Background information adequate

____ Education described

____ Achievements

    ____ of the spirit

    ____ of the body

    ____ of fortune

____ Conclusion highlighting cultural values

Editing

____ All points relevant?

____ Unity of speech

Cultural Values

____ Clearly identified

____ Relevant to this audience

____ Demonstrated in the tribute

Delivery

____ Minimal use of note cards

____ Direct eye contact

____ Posture and gestures appropriate

____ Conversational and fluent   Grade ____

SPEECH ASSIGNMENT: Exemplum

Time: 3 to 5 minutes

Description: The purpose of this assignment is to tell a story to explain a proverb that reveals important values of a culture. Humor may be your best strategy.

Skills:

- Identify a cultural value.
- Use a story or example that illuminates that value.
- Begin with impact.
- Edit: use economy, unity, and definiteness of characterization
- End with impact.

Guidelines:

Locate a quotation. Consult the reference section of your library and find a book such as *Bartlett's Familiar Quotations* that classifies quotations by major theme and by author. Another option is to search for quotations on the internet.

Once you have found your quotation, develop it in four ways. Use your text, pages 162-163, for further information.

1. Describe the author or source. For author information, consult a second reference book such as an encyclopedia, a dictionary of authors, or a *Who's Who* type of book. If your source is anonymous, state that fact. However, consider adding an explanation of why you think the quotation was important enough for people to repeat so often that it has become a cultural proverb.

2. Paraphrase the quotation in your own words. Put simply, translate it into everyday English.

3. Illustrate the major point of the quotation with a narrative drawn from your personal experiences, a historical text, an inspirational book, and the like.

4. Apply the point of the quotation and the story to the audience.

EXEMPLUM: Tenacity

Quotation: "Nothing in this world can take the place of persistence. Talent will not; nothing is more common than unsuccessful people with talent. Genius will not; unrewarded genius is almost a proverb. Education will not; the world is full of educated derelicts. Persistence and determination alone are omnipotent. The slogan 'press on' has solved and will always solve the problems of the human race."

Source: Calvin Coolidge, the 30th President of the United States (1923-1929) was born July 4, 1872, in Plymouth, Vermont. The son of a village storekeeper, he graduated from Amherst College with honors, entered law and politics in Northampton, Massachusetts, and slowly but determinedly climbed the political ladder from town councilman to Governor of Massachusetts. Warren Harding chose him to be vice-president; and when Harding died in office, Coolidge became president.

Paraphrase: The most valuable attribute is persistent. A tenacious attitude takes one farther than talent, genius, or education. I agree that tenacity is vital to a person in a difficult situation or to someone who is pursuing a goal. However, Coolidge also believed that those who "press on" will solve the problems of the human race. Tenacity is not necessarily the solution to the world's problems. In fact, a persistent despot can go far with little talent or moral fiber.

Narrative: I realized the importance of tenacity when I was assigned to military duty at the Prince Sultan Air Base in the Kingdom of Saudi Arabia. First came the notification of deployment. In preparation for departure I had an anthrax shot. The actual trip was long, with stops in the United States, Germany, and finally the air base.

Our first day of work lasted 18 hours; we endured 70-hour work weeks in sandstorms and 120 degree heat. Needless to say, we daily returned to the compound exhausted. My first roommate (who will remain nameless) went crazy after two days and was sent back to the states. My only relief was with three co-workers: Boyd from Kansas, Mullins from Missouri, and Nordhoff from Illinois. Our managers worked us hard! And we took trips to the ice cream stand at the Coalition Compound on days when one of us got reprimanded at work.

This went on for three months. One day word arrived that I could leave – on my 20th birthday. The long ride home seemed somehow shorter, and a two week island vacation was my reward. A second reward was development of my character: this experience was life changing and showed me I could get through a very unpleasant situation by "pressing on."

Application: Now, most of you won't go to Saudi Arabia. However, tenacity or perseverance is important in all situations – even when there's no promise of reward. At the very least, hard times improve character.

Adapted from a speech by Bradley Christensen, George Fox University
February 2003

EVALUATION FORM: Exemplum Speech

Name ______________________________Time______ (3 to 5 minutes)

Exemplum Pattern

___ Quotation clearly stated

____ Source identified and described adequately

____ Quotation paraphrased

____ Narrative that illustrate it

____ Application to the audience

Cultural value

____ Clearly identified

____ Relevant to this audience

____ Demonstrated in the narrative

Editing

____ All points relevant?

____ Characters clearly defined

____ Unity of speech

Language

____ Constructed dialogue (if appropriate)

____ Effective placement of details

Delivery

____ Minimal use of note cards

____ Direct eye contact

____ Posture and gestures appropriate

____ Conversational

____ Fluency of thought   Grade ____

SPEECH ASSIGNMENT: Narrative Speech

Time: 3 to 5 minutes

Description: The purpose of this assignment is to tell a story with a significant core theme regarding a cultural belief, value, attitude, or action. A humorous story may present your point effectively.

Skills:

- Identify an important cultural belief, value, attitude, action.
- Use a story or example to illustrates your core idea.
- Begin with impact.
- Choose a pattern that effectively organizes the main points.
- Edit to achieve economy, unity, definiteness of characterization.
- End with impact.

Guidelines

1. Choose a narrative function--that is, decide if you want to explain a belief, provide an example, persuade your audience, or offer possibilities (see page 288 in your text) that are as yet unrealized. Remember that reinforcing a value is a form of persuasion.

2. Identify your characters. What personality characteristics do they have? How do they look? speak? act?

3. Sketch out your plot--what happens in the story? What crisis or crises do the characters face?

4. Identify the theme or major idea your story conveys.

5. Select an organizational pattern that meets your needs. Choose from the spiral pattern (text pages 158-159), the infinity loop pattern (pages 160-162), or the exemplum pattern (pages 162-163). In some speeches, the chronological pattern (pages 151-152) may be most appropriate.

6. Polish the language in your speech. Select vivid, descriptive words. Include enough details at the beginning of your speech to set your narrative in place and time. Make sure your points of conflict are described in vivid detail. Use lists and constructed dialogue between characters where appropriate.

EVALUATION FORM: Narrative Speech

Name ____Time_______ (3 to 5 minutes)

Invention

____ Purpose is clear

____ Story characters clearly defined

____ Plot developed--climax, change in characters

____ Adequate development throughout

____ Narrative merit (story is worth telling)

Cultural Significance

____ Point of story reveals significant cultural value, attitude, behavior or belief

____ Relevant to this audience

____ Demonstrated in the narrative

Disposition

____ Effective conclusion

____ Organizational pattern clear

____ Effective introduction

____ Parts of speech effectively connected

Language

____ Constructed dialogue (if appropriate)

____ Effective placement of details

____ Listing (where appropriate)

Delivery

____ Minimal use of note cards

____ Direct eye contact

____ Posture and gestures appropriate

____ Conversational

____ Fluency of thought

Grade ____

SPEECH ASSIGNMENT:
Visual Aids Speech

Time: 5 to 6 minutes

Description: This informative speech requires skillful use of audio or visual aids that support, rather than substitute for, the main ideas of the speech. Choose support such as objects, charts, videotape clips, graphs, drawings. Your instructor may require you to create your visual on the computer.

Skills:

- Fully developed introduction and conclusion
- Clearly stated main points
- Support for each main point
- Use of signposts
- Use of at least two research sources
- Skillful use of audio or visual aids

Informative Options:

Process or Demonstration A speech clarifying a process by which something is done, is created, or occurs. You may actually demonstrate the process. (See pages 000-000 in Chapter 16.) Topics should add to the knowledge of a college-level audience.

Examples: how the lottery system works; stages of grief; how to analyze handwriting; the progress of a disease; how to upgrade a computer; how to do calligraphy; the process of learning in senior adults.

Report about a Person A speech giving the main life events and accomplishments of a famous individual who has made significant contributions to society. (See pages 000-000 in the text and the sample outline that follows.)

Examples: subjects who contributed positively--or negatively--to society: Supreme Court justices, politicians, artists, entertainers, military officers, and so on make good subjects. Consider a subject from another culture or another time.

Explanation or **Description** A speech that explains a complex idea or describes a place, event, or object--how it is made, how it works, its significance, and so on. (Pages 000 and 000 give more detail.)

Examples: lucid dreaming, noninvasive medications, a wedding in another culture, a Romanian orphanage, an ostrich.

SAMPLE OUTLINE: Process Speech

Topic:	How to fill out a 1040 IRS Form
General Purpose:	To inform
Specific Purpose:	To inform my audience how to gather, report, and assess information on the 1040 form.
Central Idea:	Obtaining data, disclosing information, and assessing the aftereffects of an IRS report are the three steps in filling out a 1040 IRS form.

[Before the speech, hand every student a copy of the 1040 form. In order to have them use it only at the appropriate time, staple a piece of blank paper over it.]

I. Introduction

A. April 15--what does that date mean to you?

B. Many people dread it as the deadline for filing tax returns.

1. Everyone who receives a W-2 wage must file.

2. Even children with accumulated interest on their bank accounts must file tax returns.

3. You may be required to file now--and you most certainly will do so in the future; you will want to save money on the process.

C. I am majoring in finance, and I learned through my courses and my experience that filing a return is not as hard as others make it seem.

D. Today, I will show you how to fill out the 1040 form by collecting data, disclosing information, and assessing the aftereffects of the process.

[Display a list on a transparency previewing the three steps.]

II. Body

A. The first step, obtaining and assessing data, is probably the most difficult.

1. The most important piece of information is the W-2 Wage Statement that your employer mails in January.

2. The IRS also mails the 1040 form in a tax packet.

3. Group all other receipts of income and expenses for the year into appropriate categories.

[Display a second transparency listing possible categories: medical expenses, charitable contributions, interest on loans, etc.]

a. Save all this information and file it for at least five years.

b. Information reported on the 1040 form must have back-up support, in case of future audit.

B. The second step is to disclose all relevant information on the 1040 form.

[Display visual of 1040 form which has been transferred to a transparency; also ask listeners' to remove the cover sheet on their handouts.]

1. Report all income in the income section--even trivial amounts.
2. Add or multiply interest factors where applicable.
3. Don't skip any lines; this may cause miscalculation.
4. Be sure to sign your return; it is void with no signature.

C. Finally, determine the after-effects of your return.

1. Were you completely truthful?
    a. Would your 1040 hold up during an audit?
    b. False information may lead to a fine, even imprisonment.
2. If you expect a refund, it may take up to twelve weeks to get a check in the mail.

III. Conclusion

A. The 1040 is a standard form each American worker must file.

B. It is simple enough that you can fill it out yourself.

[Review the three steps by displaying the first list again.]

C. April 15--don't forget this date--it will never change.

D. It's a date the IRS looks forward to!

References

H & R. Block. (1989). *H & R Block 1990 income tax guide.* New York: Macmillan Publishing.

Internal Revenue Service. (1991). IRS Tax Preparation Booklet.

Sheth, S. (1991, October 18). Personal interview.

Adapted from an outline by Nila Sheth, St. John's University

SAMPLE OUTLINE: Explanatory Speech

Topic:	Music Thanatology
General Purpose:	To inform
Specific Purpose:	To inform my audience about music that's played to terminally ill patients as they die.
Central Idea:	Music thanatology—music played to dying patients--differs from music therapy; it is an ancient practice that is being revived today.

Introduction

[Turn on a CD of harp music that plays softly during the introduction.]

I. More than 1000 people die annually in Portland area hospitals; some die suddenly as a result of traumatic accidents; many others die as a result of terminal illnesses.

A. Dying patients need to be kept comfortable, so the Providence Health System recently instituted a procedure to give patients' peace at the end of their lives.

B. Music thanatology is the prescriptive use of music, typically the voice and the harp, to help aid mental, physical, and spiritual symptoms of those approaching death; the word thanatology comes from the Greek word *thanatos*, which means death.

II. Death is inevitable for us and for our loved ones, but no one wants pain and suffering when the inevitable takes place.

III. I first heard about music thanatology as a news item on the radio; my curiosity was piqued, and I wanted to know more about the technique.

IV. I will first explain the difference between music thanatology and music therapy, then I'll give a brief history of the practice and show how it is currently being revived.

Body

I. Music thanatology is not the same as music therapy.

[Visual Aid: PowerPoint list that has two columns comparing therapy to thanatology.]

A. Music therapy is designed to aid life-supporting processes, but music thanatology aims to help people "unbind" and move toward the completion of life.

B. Music therapists engage people in interactive participation, often using words; music thanatologists typically eliminate words.

C. The rhythms and beats vary; music therapy is often upbeat and peppy, but music thanatology is calm and slow.

D. Music therapy aids the quality of life; music thanatology aids the quality of death (Heather Hill Hospital and Health Partnership website, last updated January 2002).

1. Music thanatology is classified as palliative medicine; the Latin root *pallium* means "cloak" or "shelter."

a. When reasonable medical procedures have failed in an irreversible illness, caregivers must shift attention from the disease to the welfare of the person as a whole and provide palliative care.

b. The Chalice of Repose website (last updated 2001) states, "In especially difficult cases of suicide attempts, burns, organ donation, and extubation, the music vigil has created an atmosphere of beauty, peace, and reverence for all participants."

2. Thanatologists adapt their music to the individual patient's needs by using rhythms that correspond with the patients' vital signs.

a. As thanatologists learn more about the patient, such as her medication and her handling of her illness, they adapt the tone and rhythm to either calm or stimulate the patient.

b. "I've seen people whose faces are tense and uncomfortable and as the music starts, this process of relaxation begins and the tenseness rolls out of the body," nurse Bee Zollo reports (Davis, 2002).

II. Music thanatology is not a new medical technique.
[Play a chant CD softly in the background during this section, stopping before point III.]

A. According to the Heather Hill Hospital website (2002), this type of holistic healing was first employed by the monks of Cluny, France, in the eleventh century.

B. Their infirmary was concerned with helping people have a peaceful death.

1. The monks used their endless devotion to music to give comfort to those who needed it most.

2. They began to use "infirmary music," which usually consisted of Gregorian chants.

a. These chants are characterized by highly developed melodic content and lack of rhythmic accent and pulse.

b. Chants are closely related to respiration and can be connected to the brain processes and central nervous system.

III. Although it is an old practice, music thanatology all but fell into obscurity until Therese Schroeder-Sheker experienced the death of a patient while working as a nurse's aid in a geriatric home.

A. According to the *Anchorage Daily News*, February 2003, Schroeder-Sheker came into a patient's room as his lungs were filling with fluid; she instinctively put her head beside his and sang to him until he died.

1. After his death, Schroeder-Sheker began to study ways that music could aid the dying, and she turned to the harp which she thought produced the most beautiful sound.

2. This experience and her newfound learnings led to the founding of the Chalice of Repose Project and awakened the dormant practice of music thanatology.

B. The Chalice of Repose Project in Missoula, MT, a groundbreaking project in the field of music thanatology, uniquely integrates palliative patient care into a graduate level educational program.

1. The Chalice of Repose's School of Music Thanatology is not affiliated with any university.

2. The program mirrors many European educational programs by offering a rigorous training experience rather than traditional classroom study.

3. Graduates receive a Practitioner Certificate and can work as paid musical clinicians.

4. The Chalice of Repose does not claim religious affiliation; instead, it embraces the concept of holistic spirituality.

    a. Students learn various faiths' philosophies and perception of death.

    b. They can relate to each patient's emotional and spiritual struggle as death approaches.

C. Currently, two full-time music thanatologists work at St. Vincent Hospital and the Portland Medical Center; also, Sacred Heart Hospital in Eugene employs music thanatologists.

1. Laura Moya was recently featured on an August 2001segment of *Oregon Public Radio.*

    a. Although only a few studies confirm the benefits of music therapy, Moya believes music can actually help a patient's oxygen saturation go up and his blood pressure stabilize.

    b. St. Patrick's Hospital and Health Sciences Center in Missoula, Montana, similarly says patients experience decreased pain, reduced anxiety, and deep slumber (www.saintpatrick.org/chalice).

        1) The music provided at Kathleen Corcoran's bedside in Eugene, Oregon, encouraged her friends and family to sit by her bedside, "pour out their hearts, and verbally express themselves," according to Sister Vivian Ripp, a music thanatologist.

        2) Each person thanked Kathleen for what she had brought into their lives, the *Eugene Register-Guard* reported (1998).

    c. Music thanatology has proven effective with a variety of conditions including cancer, respiratory and infectious diseases, AIDs, dementia, Alzheimer's, and multiple sclerosis.

    d. Laura Moya loves her work, but admits that each vigil (she has attended over 450) is emotional and usually sad; she copes by putting her emotions back into the music.

Conclusion

[Play the opening CD of harp music.]

I. Today we have looked at the ancient but also contemporary practice of music thanatology as a way of assisting dying patients.

II. We contrasted it with music therapy, noted its roots in medieval infirmaries, and heard some of its proponents' claims.

III. Death is inevitable, but music thanatologists do their best to soothe and comfort those who are going through it.

References

Chalice of Repose, Missoula, MT. (last updated 2001). Accessed online at www.chaliceofrepose.org

Davis, D. (2002, December 2). Prescriptive music. *Santa Fe New Mexican.* Accessed online at http://www.music-thanatologyassociation.com/NewFiles/Press%20Reviews/PrescriptiveMusic.html

Heather Hill Hospital and Health Partnership, Geauga County, OH. (2002). Available online at www.heatherhill.org.

McCowan, K. (1998, December 24). An exceptional death recalled. *The Register-Guard, Eugene, OR.* Accessed online at www.music-thanatologyassociation.com/NewFiles/Press%20Reviews/Sister%20Vivian%20Ripp.html.

Moya, L. (2001, August). Interview. *Oregon Public Broadcasting.* AM 550.

Music Thanatology Association International. (Accessed 2003, February 28). Available online at www.music-thanatologyassociation.com

Potempa, A. (2003, February 23). Soothing strings: Hospitals musical vigils may help ease passage for dying patients. *Anchorage Daily News*, Anchorage, AK. Accessed online at www.adn.com/epicks/story/2670851p-2707209c.html

Saint Patrick's Hospital and Health Sciences Center. Missoula, MT. Available online at www.saintpatrick.org/chalice.

Abby Rine, George Fox University

EVALUATION FORM: Visual Aids Speech

Name ________________________________Time_______

Disposition

____ Attention gained

____ Related to audience

____ Credibility established

____ Previewed

____ Organization clear

____ Main points clear

____ Signalled conclusion

____ Tied to introduction

____ Summarized

____ Ended with impact

Invention

____ Topic of significance (need)

____ Informative purpose

____ Audience related

____ Speaker credibility demonstrated throughout

____ Adequate supporting material

____ Evidence of research

____ All details relevant

____ VISUAL AID

Style

____ Precision of language
____ Jargon defined

Delivery

____ Voice: rate, volume, variety, quality
____ Posture and gestures
____ Other: appearance & eye contact

Memory

____ Minimal use of note cards
____ Fluency of thought   Grade _____

SELF-EVALUATION FORM

Name ________________________ Speech __________________

Write B (before), D (during) or A (after) if you experienced any of these reactions as you presented your speech.

Physical Symptoms

____ Heart pounding
____ Constriction of throat
____ Voice not normal? How? __________
____ Trembling? Where? ______________
____ Feeling too warm, face flushed, blushing
____ Dry mouth
____ Increased perspiration
____ "Butterflies" in the stomach
____ Other _______________________

Physical Preparation

____ Got a good night's sleep
____ Limited my caffeine
____ Consciously relaxed
____ Ate sensibly

Mental Preparation

____ Knew physical symptoms were normal
____ Took preparation and rehearsal time
____ Assumed my audience was positive
____ Assured myself I would do OK
____ Thought how interesting my topic was
____ Focused on my personal strengths
____ Kept the speech in perspective
____ Visualized myself giving a great speech

1. I noticed that my listeners...

2. Other speakers . . .

3. My goals for this speech were . . .

4. In this speech, my strengths and weaknesses were . . .

5. My instructor can help me improve by . . .

SPEECH ASSIGNMENT: Definition Speech

Description: Words are symbols in the code called language that allows humans to communicate. Words as symbols have meaning only because a group of people agree that the symbols represent an object, thought, or feeling. Often we hear the phrase, "Meanings are in people, not in words." Even within the same cultural context, you'll find many variations in the meaning of a single word.

You may choose to define a word or term from another language, a term with no exact equivalent or translation directly into U. S. English.

Skills:

- Define an abstract term so that its meaning and your interpretation of that meaning become clear to your audience.
- Clearly define the term in a well-organized manner based on careful and thoughtful analysis.

Guidelines

Main Point I: Focus on the denotation of the term found in various reference books such as a thesaurus or etymological dictionary
One of your references must be the *Oxford English Dictionary* or any unabridged dictionary.

1. You must select two of the following methods of defining a term.
    - Synonym and antonym.
    - Use and function.
    - Etymology and historical example.
    - Comparisons.

Main Point II: Focus on the connotation of the term according to your own life experience. Be as creative as you wish in clarifying the term.

1. Option: explain what the term means to you based on a personal experience.

2. Option: quote other people as to what the term means to them.

3. Additional options:
    - Telling a story.
    - Giving examples.
    - Referring to a person who exemplifies the term.
    - Relating the term to a political, social, or moral issue.
    - Anything else you can think of that may give your audience greater insight into the meaning of the word.

Beth Von Till and associates at San Jose State University.

SAMPLE SPEECH: ENDURANCE

Effie Mills, George Fox University

When you think of the word ENDURANCE, the image of a marathon runner enduring a 26-mile course is probably what comes to mind. But *Webster's Dictionary* defines it as "a bearing or suffering; a continuing under pain or distress without resistance or without sinking or yielding to pressure; sufferance; patience." The *Encarta Dictionary* says the word endurance came from the 14th century French word *endurer* which in turn came from the Latin root word *durus* which means hard.

In order to explain what the word Endurance means to me I need to describe a surgery I recently went through because of TMJ. TMJ is a very painful condition in which the jaw joint deteriorates and can't work properly. I had to have bite plane and braces before I could under go the surgery, which gave me time to come to grips with the surgery process. My oral surgeon explained how they would reconstruct my joints then cut and extend my lower jaw to prevent future problems. I would also be having my wisdom teeth removed during the same process. After surgery, my jaw would be wired shut for two months while things healed.

Unfortunately, my head knowledge did not prepare me for the reality of the experience. What should have been a four-to-five hour surgery became nine. Waking up from anesthesia was terrifying. I could hear people talking to me telling me to do different things, but I was unable to open my eyes or respond in any way. I had black-outs and nausea even after I came home. The eight weeks on baby food, soup broth, and milkshakes quickly went from "doable" to "an eternity." I changed from sleeping on my side to sleeping in a recliner at a 45degree angle.

Some of this ordeal took place over the summer, but two weeks overlapped with the beginning of my senior year in high school. During that time I sipped liquids or squirted baby food into my mouth with a syringe.

Even after my jaw was unwired, there were experiences I wasn't prepared for. As the wires came off, I felt like my jaw would fall apart. I wasn't allowed to chew for a year which meant everything I ate went through the food processor first. Imagine what that meant for parties, school lunches, and Thanksgiving and Christmas dinners. When I was finally able to chew again, I had to relearn the process. I had to start slow with only softer foods and even had to consciously make myself chew or I'd forget and just swallow.

There were definitely times that I wanted to give up. But, logically, that was impossible. So I made the best of the situation – trying to keep a positive attitude. This was not something I could control, so why fight it?

There were benefits to this process. My constant jaw pain is gone; my faith increased; I learned that I can't control everything. I also grew a lot as a person and discovered important lessons. Once my friends saw me wired shut and swollen up like a chipmunk, I was no longer too concerned about my image!

As a result of this experience, my definition of ENDURANCE is not letting the inevitable beat you; instead, rise above it for the better.

EVALUATION FORM: Definition Speech

Name ________________________________

Word Selected ____________________________

Invention and Disposition

___ Strong opening statement

___ Denotative definition

  ___ Dictionary definition

  ___ 1st method of definition

  ___ 2nd method of definition

___ Connotative definition

  ___ Term related to speaker

  ___ Interpretation clearly illustrated

___ Memorable ending

Style

___ Language appropriate

___ Concise

___ Interesting language

Delivery

___ Eye contact

___ Gestures

___ Extemporaneous delivery

Memory

___ Evidence of rehearsal

___ Minimal use of note cards

Grade _____

SPEECH ASSIGNMENT: Audiotaped Speech

Description: You will audiotape a speech. Because taped speeches--such as radio commentaries--often occur within exact time limits, your instructor may ask you to time the speech at exactly 1, 2, or 3 minutes in length.

Skills

- Effective use of vocal variety.
- Manuscript delivery, read in a conversational manner.
- (opt.) Exact timing

Guidelines

1. Choose an assignment in this workbook or from the text, Appendix B. An announcement, tribute, speech of definition, exemplum, farewell, or introduction work well.

2. Organize your speech carefully according to guidelines given in the text or workbook. Pay special attention to connectives.

3. (Opt.) Edit your material so that it is exactly one *or* two *or* three minutes in length.

4. Write out your speech using capital letters and triple spacing.

5. Because you must convey shades of meaning through vocal variation alone, pay special attention to pauses, accents, rate, and volume to enhance your message. Then mark your script accordingly.

    - Circle or use a colored highlighter on words you plan to stress.
    - Put // (slash) marks where you intend to pause.
    - Put a ≠ where you want your tone to rise and a Ø where you want it to fall.
    - Practice reading the script until you're satisfied that your delivery sounds conversational--as if you're conversing with only one person. Mentally visualize a typical listener, then speak directly to that individual.

6. Practice reading your script until you're satisfied that your delivery sounds conversational. Speak as if you were conversing with only one person. Mentally visualize a typical listener, then speak directly to that individual.

7. Tape record your speech. Replay the tape, listening carefully to your voice. If you don't like what you hear, simply re-record the speech until you are satisfied.

8. Bring the tape to class, cued up to the beginning of your final version.

EVALUATION FORM: Audiotaped Speech

Name ____________________________Time____________

Invention

___ Appropriate topic

___ Purpose clear

___ Main ideas clear

___ Main ideas supported

Disposition

___ Organizational pattern clear

___ Transitions, internal previews and summaries

___ Effective introduction

___ Strong conclusion

Style

___ Language appropriate, clear

___ Interesting language

Delivery

___ Appropriate rate

___ Volume

___ Vocal variety

___ Effective use of pauses

___ Conversational delivery

Grade ____

SPEECH ASSIGNMENT: Thirty-Second Videotaped Speech

Description: Prepare and videotape a thirty-second speech. You can find this type of speech on some local news broadcasts that allow citizens to voice their opinions in short speeches.

Skills:

- Choose an appropriate speech purpose--to convince, reinforce,
- inform, or actuate your audience.
- Deliver a speech effectively using cue cards or a TelePrompTer.
- Use nonverbal skills to deliver your speech effectively on camera.
- Edit your material to fit precisely into a time frame.

Guidelines:

1. Choose a single idea that you can convey in a short period of time.

   Examples of TV editorials: A woman who had adopted racially mixed children told the audience that she is happy to discuss adoption, but urged them not to ask, "Where did you get your children?" in the child's presence. A man urged people not to purchase a book by a convicted criminal. He argued that people shouldn't profit from their crimes.

   Examples of student topics: One announced a community clean up day and urged the audience to participate in it. Another reinforced the cultural value of reaching out to others by urging listeners to donate to the food bank. A third student rhymed his speech urging the audience to put on shorts and enjoy the last few days of autumn.

2. Organize your ideas. The single point speech (Chapter 2 in this workbook), a simplified Monroe's Motivated Sequence (page 334 in the text), or one of the speeches in Appendix B are appropriate.

3. Edit your speech to exactly thirty seconds. Transfer your script to a TelePrompTer, if one is available. If not, use large cue cards that you read as someone holds them near the camera.

4. Videotape your speech, using the cue cards or a TelePrompTer.

5. After you view all the speeches in the class, discuss the following questions:

6. What was the easiest part of this assignment? What was most difficult?

7. What topics did you consider and discard as possibilities? Why?

8. What can be "covered" in 30 seconds? What cannot?

SAMPLE THIRTY-SECOND SPEECH: Tinnitis

Patrick Barbo modified his longer speech on tinnitis for this short speech.

YOU ONLY HAVE TWO HANDS, AND I BET YOU DON'T TAKE A HAMMER AND SLAM THOSE HANDS EVERYDAY THEN EXPECT THEM TO WORK PROPERLY.

SIMILARLY, YOU ONLY HAVE TWO EARS. YET MOST PEOPLE SLAM THEM EVERYDAY WITH LOUD NOISE WITHOUT EVEN THINKING TWICE ABOUT POSSIBLE PERMANENT DAMAGE BEING DONE.

TURNING DOWN THE VOLUME ON YOUR MUSIC CAN REDUCE SOME DAMAGE TO YOUR HEARING.

IMAGINE YOURSELF AS AN OLDER PERSON WITH PERMANENT WHISTLING IN YOUR EARS, THEN IMAGINE YOURSELF WITHOUT HEARING PROBLEMS.

YOU CHOOSE. IT'S UP TO YOU TO KEEP THE VOLUME DOWN NOW TO AVOID PROBLEMS LATER.

EVALUATION FORM: Thirty-Second Speech

Name ______________________________ Time ____________

Invention and Disposition

___ Topic appropriate to the time limit

___ Purpose clear

___ Major idea clear

___ Supporting material to the point

___ Organized well

___ Edited well

Style

___ Language appropriate, clear

___ Interesting language

Delivery

___ Timing

___ Pleasant facial expressions

___ Appropriate gestures

___ Camera-appropriate clothing

___ Camera-appropriate grooming

___ Vocal variety

___ Appropriate speaking rate

___ Volume

___ Conversational-sounding delivery Grade ____

SELF-EVALUATION FORM

Name ________________________ Speech __________________

Write B (before), D (during) or A (after) if you experienced any of these reactions as you presented your speech.

Physical Symptoms

____ Heart pounding
____ Constriction of throat
____ Voice not normal? How? __________
____ Trembling? Where? ______________
____ Feeling too warm, face flushed, blushing
____ Dry mouth
____ Increased perspiration
____ "Butterflies" in the stomach
____ Other ________________________

Physical Preparation

____ Got a good night's sleep
____ Limited my caffeine
____ Consciously relaxed
____ Ate sensibly

Mental Preparation

____ Knew physical symptoms were normal
____ Took preparation and rehearsal time
____ Assumed my audience was positive
____ Assured myself I would do OK
____ Thought how interesting my topic was
____ Focused on my personal strengths
____ Kept the speech in perspective
____ Visualized myself giving a great speech

1. I noticed that my listeners . . .

2. Other speakers . . .

3. My goals for this speech were . . .

4. In this speech, my strengths and weaknesses were . . .

5. My instructor can help me improve by . . .

SPEECH ASSIGNMENT: Current Issue Speech

Time: 6-7 min.

Description: Think of this speech as an investigative news report. Select a current problem or controversial topic and present it as objectively as you can. Visual aids may accompany this speech in a supporting role.

Consult at least three sources for this speech--one from within the last six months. (An "A" speech should have seven sources.) Be prepared to discuss any source you cite or list on your bibliography.

Skills:

- Informative purpose
- Invention: examples, statistics, testimony, audience analysis, speaker credibility, cited sources from library research
- Disposition: use of transition statements, internal preview/ internal summary. All organizational skills from the audio-visual speech.
- Style: language that is accurate, appropriate, clear, and interesting
- Delivery: extemporaneous delivery from a key word outline

Guidelines:

Invention. Topic choice sometimes causes stress. Select a subject that doesn't bore you to sleep, but one that does not make you so angry you cannot present an informative speech. Because of the nature of the assignment, you will probably not be an "expert."

1. Read newspapers, news magazines, and other sources such as the Voter's Pamphlet. Broadcasts such as the *NewsHour* with Jim Lehrer (PBS) or *All Things Considered* (National Public Radio) include more in-depth coverage than the typical network shows.

2. Present information that is not widely known. Most people know all they care to about abortion and other common controversial topics.

3. Do research using current oral, print, or electronic materials. Define the problem. Identify its components. Gather statistics, examples, and testimony to support your main points.

Disposition. Select an organizational pattern that will help the audience get the most from your speech. Pro/con is often effective.

1. Write your intro. Gain attention & reveal your topic. Relate to the audience. Provide your qualifications for this topic. Preview your main points.

2. Write your conclusion. Signal the end is near. Review main points. Refer to the introduction. Provide a memorable ending.

3. Polish the speech by writing transition statements, internal summaries and/or internal previews.

4. Outline the speech, writing rhetorical labels in the margin. Type and proofread your work.

Style. Evaluate word choices and word combinations. Choose vivid words. Check pronunciation of words of which you are unsure.

Memory and Delivery. Put speaking outline on note cards. Write single cue words only--no complete sentences. Practice the speech. Time yourself. Edit.

EVALUATION FORM: Current Issue Speech

Name ____________________________________Time_________

____ Topic choice (significant)
____ Informative purpose

Disposition

____ Attention gained
____ Related to audience
____ Established credibility
____ Previewed

____ Organization clear
____ Main points clear
____ Main points supported
____ Transition/internal summary/preview

____ Signaled speech conclusion
____ Tied to intro
____ Review of main points
____ Ended memorably

Invention

____ Adequacy of support
____ Statistics
____ Example
____ Testimony
____ Relevant data
____ Cited sources

Style

____ Precise language
____ Vivid style

Memory

____ Evidence of practice
____ Fluency of thought
____ Minimal use of notes

Delivery

____ Voice: rate, pitch variation, volume, pauses
____ Eye contact
____ Posture
____ Gestures

Grade ____

SPEECH ASSIGNMENT: Persuasive Speech

Time: 6 to 7 minutes

Description: The purpose of this speech is to alter or reinforce attitudes, values, beliefs, or actions.

Skills:

- All previous skills of invention and disposition
- Use of proofs: audience (pathos), speaker (ethos), and rational (logos)

Examples of Persuasive Topics and Purposes:

To actuate behavior: The average American's junk mail adds up to 1 1/2 trees worth of paper annually; save trees by writing to a specific address and having your name removed from junk mail lists.

To convince/policy: Because Americans need to conserve fossil fuels, and because cars automobiles get better gas mileage at slower speeds, the nation should return to the 55 mph speed limit.

To convince of a value: Educational choice is good, because it allows people to have personal control over their lives.

To reinforce a belief or value: Democracy continues to be the best system of government in the world today.

Guidelines:

1. Select a topic, using the suggestions found on pages 378-379 of the text. What do you believe or feel strongly about? What will create a better society or better, more fulfilled individuals?

2. Decide on a claim of fact, value, or policy.

3. Analyze your audience's current beliefs and behaviors, attitudes and values as they relate to your topic.

4. Plan how you will intertwine appeals to logic, to emotion, and to your credibility in order to be more persuasive.

5. Choose an organizational pattern that is appropriate for the subject matter and purpose of your speech. Prepare an introduction, conclusion, and connectives that make your speech "flow."

6. Pay attention to language choices, checking for clarity, accuracy, and interest.

7. Outline the contents of your speech. Type your outline. Make a speaking outline on note cards using key words only.

8. Rehearse.

SAMPLE OUTLINE: Persuasive Speech to Actuate

Topic:	Organ Donation
General Purpose:	To persuade
Specific Purpose:	I will prove that there is a shortage of organs in the United States that can be eliminated if individuals will donate their organs.
Central Idea:	A shortage of organs exists in the U. S., but we can solve the problem if each person agrees to donate.

I. Introduction

A. At eighteen, Kevin, the high achiever of his senior class, had a bright future when he suddenly died of a brain aneurysm.

1. His parents faced a choice thrust upon thousands of families: to keep Kevin's body functioning long enough for transplant teams to remove his organs, corneas, and bone marrow, or to allow him simply to die.

2. Kevin's parents chose to donate his organs—fortunately, an increasingly common practice.

B. There is a nationwide shortage of available organs; you or one of your loved ones may join the thousands of people desperately need transplants.

C. I became interested in this subject this summer when my cousin was hit in the head with a baseball and declared brain dead; his organs were removed and flown to various parts of the U. S. to give renewed life to many people.

D. Today, I'll discuss the problem of organ scarcity and its causes; then I will show how each of you can be part of the solution.

II. Body

A. Organ donating is basically a problem of supply and demand.

1. Every day 80,000 people wake up needing an organ donation.

a. During the day, 66 of them will receive a transplant, 17 will die, and 115 names will be added to the list.

b. Obviously, there is a "brutal imbalance of supply and demand" according to *U.S. News & World Report*, January 13, 2003.

2. Thousands more, not yet critically ill, could benefit from new organs (Carey, 1989, p. 96).

a. According to *Science News* (Weiss, p. 348), one type of chronic leukemia will eventually kill most of its sufferers, unless they receive a complete replacement of their cancerous bone marrow.

b. About 1/2 of the 500 infants who need liver transplants each year die waiting for an organ to become available (Carey, 1989, p. 96).

c. According to American Kidney Fund Web page (accessed March 1, 2003) nearly 45,000 people are waiting for kidney transplants; only 12,000 will get them.

B. It is easy to see that there are not enough organs, and there are several reasons for this.

1. According to a Gallup survey 85% of respondents approved of organ donation, but only 69% said they were likely to donate; 25% said they were very unlikely to do so – and 47% of these people gave no reason or said they had given the matter little thought (2000).

2. Another cause of the shortage may be reluctance to deal with death.

a. Some don't sign donor cards, nor do they urge family and friends to do so, simply because they want to think about dying.

b. Some believe the remains of the dead should lie intact (Colen, 1989).

3. Dean Kappel of the Mid-America Transplant Association says that doctors and nurses are reluctant to get involved (Maier, 1990).

a. Some feel uncomfortable imposing on grieving families.

b. No physician will consider transplantation without consent of next-of-kin--even if the patient had a donor card, due to fear of lawsuits.

4. A lesser factor is the fear that someone will terminate life-supports inappropriately to take organs (Colen, 1989).

5. All of these reasons contribute to the shortage of organs; as Julia French of the American Council on Transplantation says, "It's terrible to know that the technology exists to save your life or the life or one of your family members and you don't have access to it" (Carey, 1989, p. 94).

6. Many people do not realize that, with advances in medical science, they don't have to die to donate.

a. In 2001, 6485 living donors provided bone marrow, kidneys, and other organs.

b. In April 2001, Secretary Thompson launched a national campaign to encourage Americans to "Donate the Gift of Life" (2002).

TRANSITION: Although there is a desperate shortage right now, it doesn't have to be that way.

C. Nearly 70 organs and non-organs can be donated (Richmond, 1990).

1. Donations include: skin grafts to burn victims, heart valves, corneas, ligaments, and even bone.

a. 6000-7000 people who need marrow transplants each year don't have a sibling with a similar marrow type (Slom, 1990); you can donate bone marrow any time, like you donate blood.

b. The average bone donor can help 51 people.

2. The federal Department of Human Health and Services organ donor Web site (2003) says you must tell your family of your desire to be a donor.

    a. In most states, drivers licenses contain check-off boxes for those who desire to donate.

    b. Carrying an organ-donor card or writing a living will can accomplish the same purpose.

    c. Let your family know; most states and the District of Columbia have passed "required request" laws that mandate doctors to ask survivors about organ donation when appropriate (Colen, 1989).

3. "This is something much deeper than an act of civic duty or the exchange of a commodity," says David Thomas, Director of Medical Humanities at Loyola University. "It is a profoundly spiritual act that recognizes that all human beings have an obligation to help another" (Maier, 1990, p. 110).

TRANSITION: If these are followed through, it will be possible to give someone with failing organs a second chance with minimal costs and multiple benefits.

D. The solution is practical.

1. Reassure your family that there is no financial cost and no disfigurement in case of an open-casket funeral (Richmond, 1990).

2. Giving may even benefit the family.

    a. Transplant coordinators say the act of giving marks the first step in successful grieving.

    b. It helps many families find meaning in tragic death.

        1) "For me the decision brought comfort, not more pain," says Peggy Bishop whose three-year-old son died of a cerebral hemorrhage. "My son turned out to be a gift of life to five other families" (Maier, 1990, p. 111).

        2) Nine out of ten donor families would make the same decision again (Maier, 1990).

3. Success rates are high in transplantation.

    a. 91-96% of kidney recipients, 80% of heart recipients, and 65-70% of liver transplant patients survive for at least a year after the donation according to *McCalls'* (Slom, 1990, p. 42).

    b. Less than 20% of patients with diseased marrow survive without a transplant; 70% survive with new marrow.

4. More kidney transplants would cut high health care expenditures.

    a. According to the Annenberg Washington Program at Northwestern University, follow-up costs after a $32,000 kidney transplant are only about 1/3 the cost of continued dialysis.

b. This would save $25,000 per patient per year (Rothfeder, 1989, p. 94).

5. People used to worry that donated organs would go only to important, wealthy, or well-connected people.

a. In 1984, the National Organ Transplant Act set up a nationwide computerized system to which all transplant centers connect.

b. It matches donors and recipients based on location, tissue, blood type, body size, and urgency (Rothfeder, 1989, p. 95).

6. As you can see, the cost is minimal; the savings are great.

III. Conclusion

A. I hope you now realize what a desperate need there is for organs, why there is a shortage, what can be done to solve the problem, and the many benefits that come from donating.

B. I want you all to get out your driver's licenses when you get home, look at the little box in the corner, and see if there is a "D" for DONOR.

1. If not, go to the DMV and get a donor card.

2. More importantly, tell your family that you want to be a donor and encourage them and others to donate, too; although licenses are legal documents, doctors always discuss the issue of donation with family members (Myths and Facts, 2003).

C. Several weeks after his death, Kevin's parents received a letter telling them who had benefited from their generosity.

1. One kidney went to a 37-year-old woman; the other, to a 37-year-old man.

2. Kevin's liver saved the life of a Minnesota mother of two teenagers.

3. His heart went to a 14-year-old, dying of heart disease.

4. His lungs were used in research.

5. His skin and his bone helped an undetermined number of people.

6. His corneas restored the sight of two people.

D. I strongly urge you all to donate; what greater gift can you possibly give than the gift of life?

References

Camarow, A. (2003, January 13). Transplant trauma. *U.S. News & World Report*, pp. 42-44.

Carey, J. (1989, November 27). There just aren't enough hearts to go around. *Business Week*, 94.

Colen, B. D. (1989, April 21). Desperate measures. *Health*, 84-5.

Frequently asked questions. (2003, March 1, date accessed). HHS organ donor Web site. http://www.organdonor.gov/faq.html.

Gallup Survey (2000, May 11). American public's attitudes toward organ donation and transplantation. Accessed online at www.transweb.org/reference.

"Gift of Life" Donation Initiative. (2002, April 22). Department of Health and Human Services. http://www.hhs.gov/news/press/2002pres/20020422.html

Important facts about kidney disease. (2002, March 1, date accessed). American Kidney Fund. Accessed online at http://www.akfinc.org/KidneyFacts/KidneyFacts.htm.

Maier, F. (1990, March). A final gift. *Ladies Home Journal*, 107, 102.

Myths and facts. (2003). Donate life: Coalition on donation Web site. Accessed online at http://www.shareyourlife.org/

Richmond, S. (1990, January). The gift of a better life. *Changing Times*, 44, 92-3.

Rothfeder, J. (1989, August 28). So many patients, so few donors. *Business Week*, 94-95.

Slom, C. (1992, January). Give the gift of life. *McCall's*, 117, 42.

Danielle Schutz, Oregon State University (updated 2003)

EVALUATION FORM: Persuasive Speech (General Form)

NAME ______________________________Time ________ Claim: ______________________________

Invention and Disposition

____Topic Appropriate to Audience and Time
____ Speech Purpose Clear

Introduction
_____ Attention gained
_____ Related to Audience
_____ Credibility Revealed
_____ Preview

Body
_____ Clearly organized points
_____ Proofs
    _____ Pathos: audience appeals
    _____ Ethos:
    _____ Rational proofs
    _____ Supporting evidence
_____ Adequacy of data/claims/warrants
_____ Evidence of research (sources)
_____ Ethics of argument
_____ Transition statements

Conclusion
_____ Signal of end
_____ Review of main points
_____ Tie to introduction
_____ Impact ending/call to action

Style

_____ Language appropriate
_____ Vivid language
_____ Clarity

Delivery

_____ Vocalics: rate, volume, variation, quality
_____ Pronunciation
_____ Body language: posture, gestures, eye contact
_____ Other: appearance, space, time

Memory

_____ Fluency of thought
_____ Minimal use of notes

Grade ______

EVALUATION FORM: Monroe's Motivated Sequence

Name ______________________________________Time______

Claim: ____

Invention and Disposition

I. Attention Step (Introduction)

____ Attention
____ Related to audience
____ Credibility established
____ Previewed

II. Need Step

____ Problem demonstrated
____ Ramifications given
____ Use of sufficient support
____ Pointing to audience need

III. Satisfaction Step

____ Solution described
____ Solution explained
____ Need and solution logically connected
____ Practicality of solution
____ Objections met

IV. Visualization Step

____ Hypothetical positive results
____ Hypothetical negatives if not implemented
____ Contrast

V. Action Step

____ Summarized
____ Called for response
____ Stated personal intention
____ Ended with impact

Style ____ Vivid language
____ Clarity

Delivery/Memory

____ Vocalics: rate, volume, tone, quality
____ Body language: posture, gestures
____ Other nonverbal: appearance, space, time
____ Minimal use of notes
____ Eye contact

Grade _____

Panel Discussion: A Current Controversial or Problematic Issue

Time: 20-25 minutes.

Description: You will work with a group to discuss a controversial or problematic topic in depth in an informal "fishbowl" setting with other members of the class observing.

Skills:

- All of the abilities of invention, disposition, style, and delivery from previous speeches.
- Ability to cooperate with a group to discuss a problem in depth.

Guidelines:

1. Choose an interesting topic that represents a problem on the campus, local, national, or international level.
2. Meet with a small group of people who share your interest in the topic, and divide up areas of the topic to research individually.
3. Gather information, using the worksheets that follow. In an "A" level discussion, each participant should find 5-7 items from newspapers, magazines, books, Internet sources, interviews, and the like.
4. Meet with your fellow panelists to discuss your information in depth.
5. Decide on the questions your group will discuss.
6. Select one person to act as emcee. She or he should do as much research as other panelists and prepare by sharing information with others. See the role description below.

Participants Should:

- Listen without interrupting (even if they violently disagree).
- Avoid a discussion between two people only; this is not a conversation.
- Make comments relatively brief.
- Ask fair, brief, and clear questions of other participants.
- Speak to the point of the issue being discussed at the moment.
- Be courteous to other participants.

The Emcee Should:

- Be familiar with the subject.
- Prepare a tentative outline to cover the main phases of the problem.
- Introduce the topic, relates it to the audience, and previews the discussion.
- Act as gatekeeper who invites all panelists to participate about equally, preventing one or two people from dominating the discussion.
- Keep the discussion on course.
- Summarize, when appropriate, the points on which discussants agree.
- Harmonize areas of disagreement.
- Conclude the discussion with a summary.

Topic Examples

media violence
grade inflation
male-female differences
castration for rapists
homeschooling
"repressed memory syndrome"
alternative medicine
the "three strikes and you're out" policy

A group of students discussed the problem of campus parking. They followed the problem solving method shown in the textbook, pages 000-000. In a panel format, they:

defined the problem
analyzed related facts, causes, effects, values, and policies
discussed criteria for a solution
listed possible solutions
and argued for construction of a new parking garage as the best possible solution

Another group did an investigative report on immigration issues, including the history of immigration, global immigration, political asylum, the positive effects of immigrants on the United States, the cost of immigrants to taxpayers.

Group Presentation: Movie Reality vs. Print Reality

presentation to last approximately 20 minutes

Description: Historical narratives often make good movie plots. Consequently, you can find a number of films based on historical events or characters. Working with a group, watch a movie that's based on history, then do research to evaluate the movie's accuracy. Present your findings to your classmates in a panel or symposium format.

Skills:

- All of the skills of invention, disposition, style, and delivery from previous speeches.
- Research into movie reviews, historical texts, and the like.
- Ability to compare and contrast movie reality and print reality.
- Ability to cooperate with a group to discuss a problem in depth.

Guidelines:

1. Select a historical movie that interests you and make arrangements for your group to watch it--preferably together.

2. Locate three (for a "C"), five (for a "B") or seven (for an "A") related print sources per group member. Photocopy, take notes, make a mindmap or otherwise record your findings.

3. Meet with your group and discuss your information thoroughly. Identify questions or gaps in your information that require further research. Plan additional library research and group meetings as needed.

4. Work with your group and plan a way to present your findings to the rest of the class. You may divide up the topic and have each member present one aspect of it. Or you may present your information in a panel format. Don't overlook the use of visual aids, including brief clips from the movie that illustrate your major points.

5. Participate in the group presentation.

6. Prepare a written summary of your findings, complete with a bibliography.

Topic Ideas:

Movies about people: Evita Peron (recently starring Madonna and earlier Fay Dunaway as Evita), Samson and Delilah, Truman, Nixon, Patton, Dorothy Parker, Franklin and Eleanor Roosevelt, Malcolm X, Gandhi, Eric Liddell ("Chariots of Fire").

Movies about events: "All the President's Men" (Whitewater), "JFK" (the assassination plot), "Mississippi Burning" (civil rights workers murdered), the sinking of the Titanic, "Raid over Entebbe" (the Israeli army rescue of hostages in 1976).

NOTE: Controversial movies work well.

I highly recommend "JFK" because it was released with enormous amounts of press coverage. Critics accused filmmaker Oliver Stone of everything from propaganda to paranoia. *Time* and *Newsweek* made the movie a cover issue. The *New York Times* presented a host of letters to the editor and related opinion pieces--including one from Oliver Stone. The *National Review* provided lengthy pieces by authors who participated in the actual events. To locate these materials, find out when the movie was released, then go to newspaper and magazine indexes from that date.

Another recommendation is "All the President's Men" because June 1997 marked the 25th anniversary of the Watergate break-in. This means that thousands of words were written during the middle of June, 1997, about the facts as well as the monumental impact of Watergate. Find a textbook or encyclopedia to get a basic overview of the events which stretched out over months. Go back to the original *Washington Post* stories--which you can discover from indexes. Do research in newsmagazines from the following months. Read Woodward and Bernstein, David Halberstam, and other media historians. Include conservative as well as more liberal sources.

EVALUATION FORM: Panel Discussion or Group Presentation

Names ____

Group Topic ____

The Group as a Whole

___ Introduction/Orientation to topic

___ Purpose of presentation clear

___ Evidence of group co-creation of meaning

___ Transitions

___ Conclusion

___ Question and answer period

Group grade ____

Individual Participation

___ Main points clear

___ Adequate support for ideas

___ Interesting (relevant)

___ Appropriate language (clear, correct, etc.)

___ Evidence of Research

___ Sources Cited

___ Extemporaneous delivery

___ Conversational

___ Eye contact

___ Vocal variation

Individual grade ____